CHRONOLOGY AND
DOCUMENTARY HAND-
BOOK OF THE STATE
OF MICHIGAN

*Seal of the State of Michigan*

# CHRONOLOGY AND DOCUMENTARY HANDBOOK OF THE STATE OF
# MICHIGAN

### ROBERT I. VEXLER

*State Editor*

### WILLIAM F. SWINDLER

*Series Editor*

1978 OCEANA PUBLICATIONS, INC./Dobbs Ferry, New York

**Library of Congress Cataloging in Publication Data**

Main entry under title:

Chronology and documentary handbook of the State
    of Michigan.

    (Chronologies and documentary handbooks of
the States; v. 22)
    Bibliography: p.
    Includes index.
    SUMMARY: Includes a chronology of events in
Michigan from 1620 to 1977, a biographical
directory of prominent citizens, and selected
documents.
    1. Michigan—History—Chronology.
2. Michigan—Biography.  3. Michigan—History—
Sources.  [1. Michigan—History]  I. Vexler, Robert I.
II. Series.
F566.5.C48        977.4'002'02        78-15754
ISBN 0-379-16147-8

Manufactured in the United States of America

# TABLE OF CONTENTS

# ACKNOWLEDGMENT

Special recognition should be accorded Melvin Hecker, whose research has made a valuable contribution to this volume.

Thanks to my wife, Francine, in appreciation of her help in the preparation of this work.

Thanks also to my children, David and Melissa, without whose patience and understanding I would have been unable to devote the considerable time necessary for completing the state chronology series.

*Robert I. Vexler*

# INTRODUCTION

This projected series of <u>Chronologies and Documentary Handbooks of the States</u> will ultimately comprise fifty separate volumes - one for each of the states of the Union. Each volume is intended to provide a concise ready reference of basic data on the state, and to serve as a starting point for more extended study as the individual user may require. Hopefully, it will be a guidebook for a better informed citizenry - students, civic and service organizations, professional and business personnel, and others.

The editorial plan for the <u>Handbook</u> series falls into six divisions: (1) a chronology of selected events in the history of the state; (2) a short biographical directory of the principal public officials, e.g., governors, Senators and Representatives; (3) a short biographical directory of prominent personalities of the state (for most states); (4) the first state constitution; (5) the text of some representative documents illustrating main currents in the political, economic, social or cultural history of the state; and (6) a selected bibliography for those seeking further or more detailed information. Most of the data found in the present volume, in fact, have been taken from one or another of these references.

The current constitutions of all fifty states, as well as the federal Constitution, are regularly kept up to date in the definitive collection maintained by the Legislative Drafting Research Fund of Columbia University and published by the publisher of the present series of <u>Handbooks</u>. These texts are available in most major libraries under the title, <u>Constitutions of the United States: National and State</u>, in two volumes, with a companion volume, the <u>Index Digest of State Constitutions</u>.

Finally, the complete collection of documents illustrative of the constitutional development of each state, from colonial or territorial status up to the current constitution as found in the Columbia University collection, is being prepared for publication in a multi-volume series by the present series editor. Whereas the present series of <u>Handbooks</u> is intended for a wide range of interested citizens, the series of annotated constitutional materials in the volumes of <u>Sources and Documents of U. S. Constitutions</u> is primarily for the specialist in government, history or law. This is not to suggest that the general citizenry may not profit equally from referring to these materials; rather, it points up the separate purpose of the <u>Handbooks</u>, which is to guide the user to these and other sources of authoritative information with which he may systematically enrich his knowledge of this state and its place in the American Union.

William F. Swindler
Series Editor

Robert I. Vexler
Series Associate Editor

*Si Quaeris Peninsulam Amoenam Circumspice/*
*If You Seek a Pleasant Peninsula, Look About You*

**State Motto**

# CHRONOLOGY

1620      Etienne Brulé explored Michigan for France.

1634      Jean Nicolet explored the Great Lakes. He reached St. Mary's Falls and discovered Lake Michigan.

1641      Two Jesuits, Rambault and Jogues, visited the site of Sault Sainte Marie where they established a mission as part of their plans to convert the Chippewas.

1659      Groseilliers and Pierre Radisson explored Lake Superior.

1668      Father Jacques Marquette founded the first permanent settlement in Michigan at Sault Sainte Marie.

1671      The mission house burned at Sault Sainte Marie. A finer edifice was constructed.

Saint Lusson took possession of the territory around Lake Huron and Lake Superior for France at Sault Sainte Marie.

Father Marquette established a mission among the Hurons at Michilimackinac.

1673      Jacques Marquette and Louis Joliet organized an expedition, which set out from St. Ignace in Canada. They sailed down the Mississippi River to the mouth of the Arkansas River.

July. Fort Frontenac was constructed.

1674      Spring At the instigation of the Crees, ten Sioux peace delegates were killed at Sault Sainte Marie, thus preventing the establishment of peace.

1675      Father Marquette died on the shores of Lake Michigan near Ludington.

1676      La Salle arrived at Fort Frontenac.

1679      René Robert Cavelieur, Sieur de la Salle, constructed a fort at the mouth of the Saint Joseph River.

1682      La Salle reached the mouth of the Mississippi River in the Gulf of Mexico and took formal possession of the country for France, naming it Louisiana in honor of Louis XIV.

1

1699            Livingstone submitted a plan to the English
                government for establishment of a post at
                Detroit.

1701            July 24.  Antoine de la Mothe Cadillac
                established a settlement at Detroit.

                October 31.  The Company of the Colony re-
                ceived a trade monopoly for Detroit.

1706            Antoine de la Mothe Cadillac returned to
                Detroit.

1710            Cadillac left Detroit.

1712            May.  The Outagamies and Mascoutins attacked
                Detroit.

1732            Beauharnais urged colonization at Detroit.

1760            November 29.  Major Robert Rogers captured
                Detroit from the French Commander Beletre.

1763            August 5 and 6.  The Battle of Bushy Run
                was fought.  Bouquet defeated the Indians.

1764            The Indian Chief Pontiac met Major Croghan
                ar Detroit.

1775            Lieutenant governor Henry Hamilton arrived
                at Detroit.

1777            July Lieutenant governor Hamilton sent out
                war parties from Detroit.

1779            DePeyster assumed command at Detroit.

1780            Patrick Sinclair constructed a fort on Mac-
                kinac Island.

1782            Henry Hamilton was appointed lieutenant
                governor at Detroit.

1783            September 3.  The Treaty of Paris was signed
                by Great Britain and the United States, end-
                ing the Revolutionary War.  Michigan became
                part of the United States

1784            January 14.  Congress issued the first or-
                dinance for the governance of the Northwest
                Territory.

                July.  Jehu Hay arrived in Detroit to take

charge of the area.

1787          April 26.  Congress passed the Ordinance
              establishing the Northwest Territory.

1793          Summer.  Beverly Randolph, Timothy Pickering
              and Colonel Brandt, representing the Con-
              federate Indians held a conference at Detroit
              with British agents.  The negotiations col-
              lapsed when the Americans refused to fix
              Ohio as the Indian boundary.

1796          July 11.  Colonel England surrendered De-
              troit to Captain Moses Porter.

              July 13.  Col. John Francis Hamtramck arrived
              in Detroit.

              August.  The British evacuated Mackinac.

              August 13.  General Anthony Wayne arrived
              at Detroit.

1800          The Territory of Indiana was established,
              including what is now Michigan.

1802          Detroit was incorporated.

1805          January 11.  The United States Congress
              created the Territory of Michigan.

              July 1.  Governor William Hull arrived.  The
              new government of the territory was organized
              by "The Governor and judges."  Hull served
              as governor of the territory until 1813.

1806          The governor and judges chartered the Bank
              of Detroit.  Congress disapproved the act
              on March 3, 1807.

1808          September.  Congress prohibited unauthorized
              banking.

1810          Population: 4,762.

1812          Mackinac was surrendered to the British.

              August 16.  General William Hull surrendered
              Detroit to the British without a struggle.

              October 1.  St. Charles County, with its seat
              at St. Charles, was created.  It was named

for Saint Charles Booromeo, Archbishop of
Milan, Cardinal, and nephew of Pope Pius
IV, who was canonized in 1610.

September 10.  Commodore Oliver H. Perry
won a naval victory on Lake Erie.  Detroit
and the rest of Michigan, except for Mackinac, again became the possessions of the
United States.

October 29.  Lewis Cass was appointed governor of Michigan Territory.  He served in the
office until August 1, 1831.

1815          September.  A peace treaty was signed with
various Indian tribes, including the Chippewas, who lived in Indiana, Ohio and Michigan.

November 21.  Wayne County was created, with
Detroit as its seat, organized in 1815.  It
was named for General Anthony Wayne, who
fought in the Revolutionary War, was a major
general and general-in-chief of the U. S.
Army, and defeated the Indians at the Battle
of Fallen Timbers.

1817          April 28.  Great Britain and the United
States signed an agreement for limiting
naval forces on the Great Lakes.

July 14.  Monroe County was established, with
Monroe as its seat.  It was named for James
Monroe, who fought in the Revolutionary War,
was a Senator from Virginia, was 12th and
16th governor of Virginia, was Secretary of
State in the administration of President
James Madison, and was 5th President of the
United States.

August 14.  President Monroe visited Detroit.

August 26.  The University of Michigania was
incorporated.

September 29.  Generals McArthur and Cass
signed a treaty with the Chippewas, Ottawas,
Potawatamies, Wyandots, Shawanoes, Delawares
and Senecas.  Land was granted to St. Anne's
Church in Detroit and to the College of Detroit.

1818          January 15.  Macomb County was established,
              with Mount Clemens as its seat.  It was
              named for Alexander Macomb, who served in
              the U. S. Army in the War of 1812 and won
              a victory at Plattsburgh, N. Y. in 1814.
              He was later comander-in-chief of the army.

              August 27.  The "Walk-in-the-Water," the
              first steamboat to sail on Lake Erie, ar-
              rived at Detroit from Buffalo.

              October 26.  Mackinac County was created,
              with its seat at St. Ignace.

1819          January 12.  Oakland County was established,
              with Pontia as its seat.

              The Bank of Michigan was established.

              Congress empowered the residents to send
              a delegate to Congress from the Territory.

1820          Population: 8,896.

              March 28.  St. Clair County, with Port Huron
              as its seat, was established.  It was or-
              ganized 1821 and was named for Arthur St.
              Clair, member of the Continental Army during
              the Revolutionary War, delegate to the Cong-
              ress, and first governor of the Northwest
              Territory.

              December 22.  Chippewa County, with its
              seat at Sault Ste. Marie, was created, effec-
              tive February 1, 1827.  It was named for
              the Chippewa Indian tribe.

1822          September 10.  The following counties were
              established: Lapeer, Lenawee, Samilac,
              Shiawassee, and Washtenaw.  Lapeer, with
              its seat at Lapeer, was organized 1835.
              Lenawee, with Adrian as its seat, was or-
              ganized November 20, 1826.  Sanilac, organized
              1848, with its seat at Sandusky, was named
              for Sanilac, an Indian chief.

              Shiawassee, organized March 18, 1837, with
              Onunna as its seat was named for an Indian
              term meaning "river that twists about."
              Washtenaw, with Ann Arbor as its seat, was
              organized November 20, 1826 and reorganized
              1829.

1823   March 3. Congress provided for the trans-
      fer of legislative power to the governor
      and a council of nine members selected by
      the President, subject to the confirmation
      of the Senate.

1824   June 7, 1824. The first Legislative Council
      met at Detroit.

1825   The Erie Canal was opened, which in combi-
      nation with the Great Lakes, provided for
      a water route to the Atlantic Ocean.

1829   July 23. William A. Burt of Mt. Vernon,
      Michigan, received a patent for the first
      typewriter, called a "typographer."

      October 29. The following counties were
      created: Barry, Berrien, Branch, Calhoun,
      Cass, Eaton, Hillsdale, Ingham, Jackson,
      Kalamazoo. St. Joseph, Van Buren.

      Barry, with Hastings as its county seat, was
      organized in 1839 and named for William Tay-
      lor Barry, Senator from Kentucky and Post-
      master General of the United States. Ber-
      rien County, organized March 4, 1831, with
      its seat at St. Joseph, was named for John
      Macpherson Berrien.

      Branch, organized 1835, was named for John
      Branch, governor of North Carolina, gover-
      nor of Florida Territory, Senator and Repre-
      sentative from North Carolina, and U. S.
      Secretary of the Navy in the Cabinet of
      President Andrew Jackson. Calhoun, with Mar-
      shall as its seat, was named for John C.
      Calhoun, Secretary of War in the Cabinet of
      President James Monroe, Vice President of
      the United States under Presidents John
      Quincy Adams and Andrew Jackson, Senator
      from South Carolina and Secretary of State
      in the administration of President John
      Tyler.

      Cass County, with its seat at Cassopolis,
      was named for Lewis Cass, 4th and 9th gover-
      nor of Michigan Territory, Secretary of
      War in the administration of President An-
      drew Jackson, Senator from Michigan, and
      later Secretary of State in the administra-
      tion of President James Buchanan.

Eaton County, with its seat at Charlotte,
was organized at Charlotte, and named for
John Henry Eaton, Senator from Tennessee,
and later Secretary of War in the administration of President Andrew Jackson.  Hillsdale
has its seat at Hillsdale.

Ingham County, with Mason as its seat, was
named for Samuel Delucenna Ingham, Representative from Pennsylvania and Secretary of
the Treasury in the Cabinet of President
Andrew Jackson.  Jackson, organized June 26,
1832 and effective August 1, 1832, with its
seat at Jackson, was named for Andrew Jackson, major general of the U. S. Army, victor
at New Orleans, and 7th President of the
United States.

Kalamazoo County, with its seat at Kalamazoo,
was organized July 30, 1830.  St. Joseph,
organized 1829, with its seat at Centerville,
was named for Joseph, the husband of the
Virgin Mary.

Van Buren County, organized March 18, 1837,
effective April 7, 1837, with its seat at
Paw Paw, was named for Martin Van Buren,
Senator from New York, governor of New York,
Vice President of the United States under
President Andrew Jackson, and 8th President
of the United States.

1830            Population: 31,639.

                January 1.  James Witherell became secretary
                and acting governor.

                A daily boat line began running between De-
                troit and Buffalo.

1831            March 2.  The following counties were estab-
                lished: Allegan, Arenac, Clinton, Gladwin,
                Gratiot, Ionia, Isabella, Kent, Livingston,
                Midland, Montcalm, Oceana, and Ottawa.

                Allegan, with its seat at Allegan, was organ-
                ized 1835.  Arenac, with its seat at Standish,
                was organized 1883.  Clinton, organized 1839,
                with its seat at St. Johns, was named for
                De Witt Clinton, governor of New York.

                Gladwin, organized 1875, with its seat at
                Gladwin, was named for Major Henry Gladwin,

who had saved Detroit in 1703.  Gratiot,
organized 1855, with Ithaca as its seat,
was named for Charles Gratiot, who fought
in the War of 1812.

Ionia, organized March 18, 1837, effective
April 7, 1837, has its seat at Ionia.  Isabella, organized 1859, with Mount Pleasant
as its seat, was named for Isabella of Cas-
tille, Queen of Spain, who financed Colum-
bus' expedition.  Kent, organized March 24,
1836, with Grand Rapids as its seat, was
named for James Kent, member of the New York
legislature and chancellor of New York.

Livingston, organized March 24, 1836, with
its seat at Howell, was named for Edward
Livingston, who served in the War of 1812
and was Secretary of State in the administration of President Andrew Jackson.  Midland
County, with its seat at Midland, was organized 1850.  Montcalm County, organized
1835, with its seat at Stantin, was named
for Louis Joseph de Saint Veran Montcalm,
brigadier general who was in command of
the French troops in Canada.  He was mortally wounded at the Heights of Abraham,
September 14, 1759.

Oceana, with its seat at Hart, was organized
1851 and reorganized 1855.  Ottawa County,
with its seat at Grand Haven, was organized
1837, and was named for the Ottawa Indian
tribe.

August 1-September 17.  Stevens T. Mason
was secretary and acting governor of the
territory.

August 6.  George B. Porter was appointed
governor of Michigan Territory in which post
he served until his death on July 6, 1834.

Kalamazoo College was founded and chartered
at Kalamazoo.

1834            July 6.  Henry D. Gilpin was appointed governor of the territory, but was rejected by
the Senate.

Stevens Thompson Mason again became acting
governor of Michigan Territory.

1835      March 28. Genessee County was established, organized March 8, 1836, with its seat at Flint.

May 11. A constitutional convention met at Detroit and adjourned on May 24.

October. The citizens adopted the constitution.

November 3. Stevens T. Mason, Democrat, became governor of Michigan and served in the office until January 7, 1840.

Albion College was established at Albion.

1836      September 4. A convention at Ann Arbor rejected the boundaries fixed by Congress.

1837      January 26. Michigan was admitted to the Union as the 26th state.

March 18. The University of Michigan received its charter in Ann Arbor as a state university. It opened in 1841 and granted its first degrees in 1845.

The state began construction of a canal at Sault Sainte Marie, but little was accomplished by 1852.

1838      January. The Michigan Central was completed, running from Detroit to Ypsilanti.

1840      Population: 212,267.

January 7. William Woodbridge, Whig, became governor of the state and served until his resignation on February 23, 1841.

1840      April 1. The following counties were established: Alcona, Alpena, Antrim, Clare, Crawford, Emmet, Huron, Iosco, Kaskaskia, Lake, Leelanau, Manistee, Mason, Mecosta, Missaukee, Montmorency, Newaygo, Ogemaw, Osceola, Oscoda, Otsego, Presque Isle, Roscommon, Tuscola, and Wexford.

Alcona has its seat at Harrisville. Alpena, whose original name was Anamickee, was changed to its present name on March 8, 1843, with its seat at Alpena. Antrim, with its seat at Bellaire, was organized in 1863. It was

named for Antrim County, Ireland.  Clare,
organized 1871. with its seat at Harrison,
was named for Clare County, Ireland.  It was
originally named Kaykakee County, and its
name was changed to Clare on March 8, 1843.

Crawford, organized 1879, with its seat at
Grayling, was named for William Crawford,
who fought in the Revolutionary War and was
captured by the Wyandot and Delaware Indians
on the Sandusky River.  They burned him to
death at the stake.  Its name was originally
Shawaho and was changed to Crawford on March
8, 1843.

Emmet, originally Tonedagana, changing to
its present name on March 8, 1843, with its
seat at Petaskey, was named for Robert Emmet, an Irish patriot and fighter who was
executed on September 20, 1803 for his part
in the Irish rebellion.  Huron County, organized in 1859, with its seat at Bad Axe,
was named for the Huron Indians.  Iosco County, originally Kanotin, and changed on March
8, 1843, which was organized 1857, with its
seat at Tawas City, was named for the Indian
word which means "shining water."  Kaskaskia,
with its seat at Kalkaska, was organized 1871.
It was formerly Wabassee County, and its name
was changed on March 8, 1843.

Lake County, originally Aishcum County, until
its name was changed on March 8, 1843, was
organized 1871.  Leelanau County, organized
February 27, 1863, with its seat at Leland,
was named for Leelanau, a Chippewa Indian
maiden.

Manistee County, with its seat at Manistee,
was organized in 1855.  Mason County, organized in 1855, with its seat at Ludington,
was named for Stevens Thompson Mason, first
and second governor of Michigan.  It was
originally Notipekago County until March 8,
1843.

Mecosta, with its seat at Big Rapids, was
organized in 1859 and named for Mecosta,
an Indian chief.  Missaukee, organized 1871,
with its seat at Lake City, was named for
Missaukee, an Ottawa Indian chief.

Monmorency County, organized May 21, 1881,

with Atlanta as its seat, was named for Lord
Raymond de Montmorency, a French soldier.
Newaygo County, organized in 1851, with White
Cloud as its seat, was named for Newaygo,
an Indian chief.

Ogemaw County, with its seat at West Branch,
was organized in 1873 and reorganized in
1875. Osceola, with Reed City as its seat,
was organized March 10, 1881. It was named
for Osceola, an Indian chief who opposed
the cession of Seminole lands to the United
States. Oscoda, with its seat at Mio,
was organized March 10, 1881.

Otsego, with Gaylord as its county seat,
was organized in 1875. It was originally
Okkudo County until its name was changed
on March 8, 1843. Presque Isle County has
its seat at Rogers City.

Roscommon, organized in 1875, with Roscommon
as its seat, was named for Roscommon County,
Ireland. It was originally Mikenauk County
until March 8, 1843. Tuscola County has its
seat at Caro.

Wexford, organized in 1869, with its
seat at Cadillac, was originally Kautawaubet
County until March 8, 1843. It was named
for Wexford County, Ireland.

Other counties created were Cheboygan, organized 1853, with its seat at Cheboygan;
Charlevoix, organized 1869, with its seat
at Charlevoix, and named for Pierre Fran-
cois Xavier de Charleroix, a Jesuit histor-
ian and explorer; and Grand Traverse, with
its seat at Traverse City. It was originally
Omeena County until April 17, 1851.

November. A part of the Michigan Southern
Railway went into operation.

1841            January 29. St. Clair County, with its seat
at Osceola, was established. It was named
for Arthur St. Clair, who fought in the
Revolutionary War and served in the Continen-
tal Congress and was first governor of the
Northwest Territory.

February 23. Lieutenant Governor James W.
Gordon, Whig became governor of the state and

served until January 3, 1842.

1842     January 3. John Steward Barry, who had been
elected in 1841, became governor of the
state and served until January 5, 1846.

1843     Delta, Marquette, and Ontonagon Counties were
created. Delta, organized in 1861, has its
seat at Escanaba. Marquette, organized May
18, 1846 and reorganized 1848, with its
seat at Marquette, was named for Jacques
Marquette, an explorer and Jesuit mission-
ary who explored the Wisconsin and Mississippi rivers with Louis Joliet. Ontonagon
County, organized May 18, 1846 and reorganized 1848, has its seat at Ontonagon.

Albion College was opened.

1844     January. The Supreme Court declared the
state banking law unconstitutional.

The Aphadelphia Phlanax was founded on
approximately 3,000 acres with almost 500
members. Hillsdale College was established
at Hillsdale and Olivet College at Olivet.

1845     March 19. Houghton County, with its seat
at Houghton, was created. It was organized
May 18, 1846 and was named for Douglas
Houghton, the first state geologist.

Mining of iron ore was begun.

Adrian College was established at Adrian.

1846     January 5. Alpheus Felch, Democrat, who had
been elected in 1845, became governor of
the state. He served in the office until
his resignation on March 3, 1847.

May 4. The Michigan legislature passed a
law which abolished capital punishment. It
was the first state to do so. The law became effective January 1, 1847.

1847     March 3. Lieutenant William L. Greenly
became governor of Michigan upon the resignation of Governor Alpheus Felch. Greenly
served in the office until the end of the
term on January 3, 1848.

1848     January 3. Epaphroditus Ransom, Democrat,

who had been elected in 1847, became governor of the state. He served in office until January 7, 1850.

1849    August 29. The Kalamazoo State Hospital for the Insane was opened.

October 27. Wabasha County, with its seat at Wabasha, was established.

Eastern Michigan University was established at Ypsilanti.

1850    Population: 397,654.

January 7. John Steward Barry, Democrat, who had been elected in 1849, became governor of Michigan. He served in the office until January 1, 1851.

June 3. A Constitutional Convention met at Lansing. It complete its work on August 15.

November 5. The citizens of the state adopted the new constitution.

1851    January 1. Robert McClelland, Democrat, who had been elected in 1850, became governor of the state. He served until his resignation on March 7, 1853.

Hope College was founded and chartered at Holland.

1852    June. The Michigan Central Railroad opened to Chicago.

1853    March 7. Lieutenant Governor Andrew Parsons, Democrat, became governor of the state upon the resignation of Governor Robert McClelland. Parsons served until January 3, 1855.

1854    July 6. Various citizens of the state met at Jackson where they formed the Republican Party.

The Michigan State Agricultural College was established. Its first classes met in 1857.

1855    January 3. Kinsley S. Bingham, Republican, became governor of the state and served in

the office until January 5, 1859.  He had
been elected in 1854.

February 10.  Kalamazoo College was chartered.

Michigan State University was established
at East Lansing.

The first Soo Canal was finished at Sault
Sainte Maire, which linked Lake Superior
with Lake Huron.

1856        The first ship travelled from Milwaukee to
            Europe via the Welland Canal.

            The State Reform School was opened at Lan-
            sing.

1857        February 17.  Bay County, with its seat at
            Bay City, was established, effective April
            20, 1857.

            February 27.  Waseca County, with its seat
            at Waseca, was created.

            March 6.  Lewis Cass became Secretary of
            State in the administration of President
            James Buchanan.

            July 6.  The Republican State Convention
            met at Jackson.

1858        January.  A separate State Supreme Court was
            organized.

            April 12.  The first United States billiard
            championship was held at Fireman's Hall in
            Detroit.  Michael J. Phelan defeated John
            Seereiter in a match which lasted 9½ hours.

            June 11.  Wadena County was established,
            with Wadena as its seat.

1859        January 5.  Moses Wisner, Republican, be-
            came governor of the state.  He had been
            elected in 1858, and he served in the office
            until January 2, 1861.

            January 7.  Muskegan County, with its seat
            at Muskegan, was created.

Adrian College was founded and chartered at Adrian.

Professor J. M. B. Sill founded the Detroit Female Seminary.

1860        Population: 749,113.

1861        January 2. Austin Blair, Republican, who had been elected in 1860, became governor of Michigan. He served in office until January 4, 1865.

February 2. The state legislature passed resolutions which claimed the supremacy of the Union.

March 11. Keweenaw County, with its seat at Eagle River, was created.

May 7. A special session of the state legislature authorized the raising of ten regiments and a loan of $1,000,000.

1863        February 27. Benzie County, with Beulah as its seat, was established. It was organized in 1867.

March 19. Menominee County was established, with Menominee as its seat. It was named for the Menominee Indian tribe.

1865        January 4. Henry H. Crapo, Unionist Republican, who had been elected in 1864, became governor of Michigan in which post he served until January 6, 1869.

February 2. The state legislature ratified the 13th Amendment to the United States Constitution.

May 11. The Fourth Michigan Cavalry captured Jefferson Davis.

1866        Holland Seminary became Hope College.

1867        January 16. The state legislature ratified the 14th Amendment to the United States Constitution.

May 15. A Constitutional Convention met at

Lansing and completed its work on August
22.  The proposed constitution was defeated
by the voters.

1868        January 16.  William Davis, a fish-market
owner in Detroit, was granted a patent for
a refrigerator car.

Wayne State University was founded and
chartered at Detroit.

1869        January 6.  Henry Porter Baldwin, Republican, who had been elected in 1868, became
governor of the state.  He served in the
office until January 1, 1873.

March 5.  The state legislature ratified
the 15th Amendment to the United States
Constitution.

1870        Population: 1,184,059.

1871        The Federal Government constructed a canal
at the St. Clair Flats.

1872        Construction of the state capitol building
at Lansing was begun.

1873        January 1.  John Judson Bagley, Republican,
who had been elected in 1872, became governor of the state.  He served until January
3, 1877.

The position of Commissioner of Railroads
was created by the state legislature.

August 27 - October 10.  A state Constitutional Convention met at Lansing.  The constitution was rejected by the voters.

Spring Arbor College was established at
Spring Arbor.

Andrews University was established at Berrien Springs, and Battle Creek College was
also founded.

The Michigan Pioneer and Historical Society
was organized.

1875        February 19.  Bargara County, with its seat
at L'Ansel, was created.  It was named for

Frederic Bargara, a priest who wrote a Chippewa grammar in 1850 and a Chippewa dictionary in 1853. He established schools for the Chippewa and Ottawa Indians in Ohio and Michigan.

October 19. Zachariah Chandler became Secretary of the Interior in the Cabinet of President Ulysses S. Grant.

1876    Calvin College was founded and chartered at Grand Rapids.

1877    January 3. Charles Miller Croswell, Republican, who had been elected in 1876, became governor of the state. He served in the office until January 1, 1881.

The University of Detroit was founded.

The Pontiac State Hospital for the Insane was organized. It was opened on August 1, 1878.

1879    The Industrial House for Girls was founded at Adrian.

1880    Population: 1,636,937.

An asylum for the insane was established at Traverse City.

1881    January 1. David Howell Jerome, Republican, who had been elected in 1880, became governor of the state and served unthe office until January 1, 1883.

The Michigan School for the Blind was established at Lansing.

1882    Professor James D. Liggett founded the Detroit Home and Day School.

1883    January 1. Josiah W. Begole, Democrat and Greenback, who had been elected in 1882, became governor of the state and served in the office until January 1, 1885.

1884    Ferris State College was established at Big Rapids.

1885    January 1. Russell Alexander Alger, Republi-

can, who had been elected in 1884, became
governor of Michigan.  He served in this
position until January 1, 1887.

March 17.  Alger County, with its seat at
Munising, was created and organized 1885.
It was named for Russell Alexander Alger,
26th governor of Michigan, later Secretary
of War under President William McKinley and
Senator from Michigan.

April 3.  Iron County, with Crystal Falls as
its seat, was created.

November 30.  The Traverse City State Hospital for the Insane was opened.

The College of Mines was established at Houghton.

The Michigan Soldiers' House was founded at
Grand Rapids.

1886        Alma College was founded and chartered at
            Alma.

1887        January 1.  Cyrus Gray Luce, Republican, who
            had been elected in 1886, became governor
            of the state, and served in the office until
            January 1, 1891.

            February 7.  Gogebic County, with its seat
            at Bessemer, was created.

            March 1.  Luce County, with Newberry as its
            seat, was established.  It was named for
            Cyrus Gray Luce, 27th governor of Michigan.

1888        January 16.  Don M. Dickinson became Post-
            master General in the Cabinet of President
            Grover Cleveland.

1890        Population: 2,093,890.

1891        January 1.  Edwin Baruch Winans, Democrat,
            who had been elected in 1890, became governor
            of Michigan and served in the gubernatorial
            office until January 1, 1893.

            May 21.  Dickinson County, with Iron Mountain
            as its seat, was established. It was named for
            Donald McDonald Dickinson, Postmaster General
            in the administration of President Grover

Cleveland.

The Detroit Institute of Technology was founded.

The Michigan Asylum for Insane Criminals was estanlished at Ionia.

1892    Central Michigan University was founded at Mt. Pleasant.

1893    January 1. John T. Rich, Republican, who had been elected in 1892, became governor of the state and served in the office until January 1, 1897.

The Michigan House for Feeble Minded and Epileptic was established at Lapeer was founded. It opened in August, 1895.

1894    The Fort on Mackinac Island was given to the state for a park.

1895    The Central Michigan Normal School was established at Mount Pleasant.

The Industrial (Reform) School for Boys was opened at Lansing.

1896    Saginaw Valley Medical College was organized.

1897    January 1. Hazen Smith Pingree, Republican, who had been elected in 1896, became governor of the state. He served in the post until January 1, 1901.

March 5. Russell A. Alger became Secretary of War in the Cabinet of President William McKinley.

Nazareth College was founded at Kalamazoo.

Grand Rapids Medical College was established.

1898    Michigan sent five regiments and the Naval Reserves to the Spanish War.

1899    Northern Michigan University was founded and established at Marquette.

Ransom E. Olds founded the first automobile manufacturing company.

1900          Population: 2,420,982.

1901          January 1.  Aaron Thomas Bliss, Republican,
             who had been elected in 1900, became gover-
             nor of Michigan.  He served in the office
             until January 1, 1905.

1903          Western Michigan University was established
             at Kalamazoo.

             The Michigan Employment Institution for the
             Blind was organized at Saginaw.

1905          January 1.  Fred M. Warner, Republican, who
             had been elected in 1904, became governor of
             the state.  He served in the office until
             January 1, 1911.

             The Western State Normal School opened at
             Kalamazoo.

             Marygrove College was established at Detroit.

             The state sanitorium was established at
             Howell.

1907          October 22.  A Constitutional Convention was
             opened at Lansing.  It adjourned on March
             3, 1908.

             A Psychopathic Hospital was established at
             Ann Arbor.

             The Michigan Railroad Commission was estab-
             lished.

1908          December 1.  Truman H. Newberry became Sec-
             retary of the Navy in the Cabinet of Presi-
             dent Theodore Roosevelt.

1910          Population: 2,810,173.

1911          January 1.  Chase S. Osborn, Republican,
             who had been elected in 1910, became governor
             of the state.  He served in the office until
             January 1, 1913.

             February 23.  The state legislature ratified
             the 16th Amendment to the United States
             Constitution.

1913          January 1.  Woodbridge N. Ferris, Democrat,

who had been elected in 1912, became governor of the state. He served in the office until January 1, 1917.

January 28. The state legislature ratified the 17th Amendment to the United States Constitution.

The Central Michigan Sanitorium for the Treatment of Tuberculosis was founded in Jerome Township.

The Michigan Farm Colony for Epileptics was established.

1914      The Ford Motor Company established a minimum wage of $5.00.

1917      January 1. Albert E. Sleeper, Republican, who had been elected in 1916, became governor of the state and served in the office until January 1, 1921.

1919      January 2. The state legislature ratified the 18th Amendment to the United States Constitution.

June 10. The state legislature ratified the 19th Amendment to the United States Constitution.

General Motors Institute was founded at Flint.

Siena Heights College was established at Adrian.

Sacred Heart Seminary College was chartered at Detroit.

1920      Population: 3,668,412.

WWJ became the first radio station in the state at Detroit.

1921      January 1. Alexander J. Groesbeck, Republican, became governor of the state. He served until January 1, 1927, having been elected in 1920.

March 5. Edwin Denby became Secretary of the Navy in the Cabinet of President Warren G. Harding.

1922        Aquinas College was founded and chartered
            at Grand Rapids.

1927        January 1.  Fred W. Green, Republican, who
            had been elected in 1926, became governor
            of the state.  He served in the office until
            January 1, 1931.

1930        Population: 4,842,325.

            Duns Scotus College was established at
            Southfield.

1931        January 1.  Wilber M. Brucker, Republican,
            who had been elected in 1930, became gover-
            nor of the state.  He served in the office
            until January 1, 1933.

            Isle Royale National Park was established.
            It contained 539,280 acres.

1932        March 31.  The state legislature ratified
            the 20th Amendment to the United States
            Constitution.

            December 14.  Roy D. Chapin became Secretary
            of Commerce in the Cabinet of President Her-
            bert Hoover.  Chapin had been Secretary
            ad interim from August 8 to December 14,
            1932.

            Lawrence Institute of Technology was estab-
            lished at Southfield.

1933        January 1.  William A. Comstock, Democrat,
            who had been elected in 1932, became gover-
            nor of the state.  He served in the guberna-
            torial office until January 1, 1935.

            April 10.  The state legislature ratified the
            21st Amendment to the United States Consti-
            tution.

1934        October 1.  Olivet College developed a new
            plan for education.  All credits, grades,
            and other elements of a traditional univer-
            sity education were eliminated.  Students
            were only required to pass general examina-
            tions and be in residence for at least three
            years.  During the mornings students were to
            participate in private study, group discus-
            sions and individual conferences.  Afternoons
            were set aside for athletic activities in

which the faculty participated. During the evenings students were to participate in debates and other intellectual or aesthetic activities.

1935        January 1. Frank D. Fitzgerald, Republican, who had been elected in 1934, became governor of the state. He served in the office until January 1, 1937.

At its meeting in Detroit the Grand Federation of Women's Clubs reversed its stand on birth control and endorsed the federal laws permitting birth-control literature to be sent through the mails.

Michigan workers formed the United Automobile Workers Union. During the next two years they used sit-ins and strikes in order to gain collective bargaining contracts.

1937        January 1. Frank Murphy, Democrat, who had been elected in 1936, became governor of the state in which position he served until January 1, 1939.

1939        January 1. Frank D. Fitzgerald, Republican, who had been elected in 1938, became governor of the state. He served for several months until his death on March 16, 1939.

January 17. Frank Murphy became Attorney General in the Cabinet of President Franklin Delano Roosevelt. Murphy had been Attorney General ad interim from January 2 to January 17, 1939.

March 16. Lieutenant Governor Luren D. Dickinson, Republican, became governor of Michigan upon the death of Governor Frank D. Fitzgerald. Dickinson served in the office until January 1, 1941.

1940        Population: 5,256,106.

1941        January 1. Murray D. Van Wagoner, Democrat, who had been elected in 1940, became governor of the state and served in the office until January 1, 1943.

April 11. The ten-day Ford Motor Company strike was settled by Governor Van Wagoner. Both Henry Ford and the CIO agreed to make concessions.

June 20.  The Ford Motor Company signed a
union shop contract with the United Automobile Workers, who were part of the C.I.O.

November 5.  Women threw eggs and tomatoes
at British Ambassador Lord Halifax in Detroit.

Mercy College of Detroit was founded and
chartered.

1942        The Cranbrook Academy of Art was established
            at Bloomfield Hills.

1943        January 1.  Harry F. Kelly, Republican, who
            had been elected in 1942, became governor of
            Michigan.  He served in office until January
            1, 1947.

1947        January 1.  Kim Sigler, Republican, who had
            been elected in 1948, became governor of
            the state and served in office until Janu-
            ary 1, 1949.

            March 31.  The state legislature ratified
            the 22nd Amendment to the United States
            Constitution.

            WWJ-TV became the first television station
            in the state at Detroit.

            Madonna College was founded and chartered
            at Livonia.

1949        January 1.  G. Mennen Williams, Democrat,
            who had been elected in 1948, became gover-
            nor of the state.  He was reelected several
            times and served in the gubernatorial office
            until January 1, 1961.

1950        Population: 6,311,766.

1953        January 21.  Arthur E. Summerfield became
            Postmaster General in the Cabinet of Presi-
            dent Dwight D. Eisenhower.

            January 26.  Charles E. Wilson was appointed
            Secretary of Defense by President Dwight D.
            Eisenhower.  Wilson assumed his office as a
            member of the cabinet on January 28.

1955   A new copper mine was opened near On-
      tonagon.

1956   April 2-3.  Several serious tornadoes hit
      parts of Michigan.

1957   The Straits of Mackinac Bridge was opened.
      Traffic could then go between Mackinaw City
      and St. Ignace.

1959   August 6.  Frederick H. Mueller became Sec-
      retary of Commerce in the Cabinet of Presi-
      dent Dwight D. Eisenhower.  Mueller had been
      Secretary ad interim from July 21, 1959 to
      August 6, 1959.

      Oakland University was established at Roches-
      ter.

1960   Population: 7,823,194.

      Grand Valley State College was established
      at Allendale.

1961   January 1.  John B. Swainson, Democrat, who
      had been elected in 1960, became governor
      of the state.  He served in the office un-
      til January 1, 1963.

      January 21.  Robert S. McNamara became Sec-
      retary of Defense in the Cabinet of President
      John F. Kennedy.

      March 8.  The state legislature ratified
      the 23rd Amendment to the United States
      Constitution.

      The citizens of the state authorized the
      calling of a state Constitutional Convention
      to revise the state constitution of 1908.

1963   January 1.  George W. Romney, Republican,
      who had been elected in 1962, became gover-
      nor of the state.  He was reelected several
      times and served until his resignation on
      January 22, 1969 when he became United
      States Secretary of Housing and Urban De-
      velopment.

      February 20.  The state legislature ratified
      the 24th Amendment to the United States
      Constitution.

The voters of the state approved the new constitution.

1964        Michigan's new constitution went into effect.

Saginaw Valley College was established at University Center.

1965        October 5. The state legislature ratified the 25th Amendment to the United States Constitution.

1966        Lake Superior State College was founded at Sault Sainte Marie.

1967        July. An eight-day riot occurred in a predominantly black section of Detroit. 43 people were killed, and approximately $45,000,000 was destroyed or damaged.

The Michigan legislature adopted a state income tax.

1968        May 16. Wilbur J. Cohen became Secretary of Health, Education and Welfare in the Cabinet of President Lyndon B. Johnson. Cohen had been Secretary ad interim since March 2, 1968.

The citizens of the state approved a $100,000,000 bond issue to be used to provide more parks and other recreational facilities, especially in the inner core areas of Detroit and other cities. The voters also approved a $335,000,000 bond issue to fight water pollution.

1969        January 20. Governor George Romney was appointed Secretary of Housing and Urban Development by President Richard M. Nixon. He assumed his office as a member of the cabinet after resigning his post as governor on January 22.

January 22. Lieutenant Governor William G. Milliken, Republican, became governor upon the resignation of Governor George Romney. Milliken served until the end of the term and was subsequently elected in 1970.

1970        Population: 8,875,083.

1971        April 7. The state legislature ratified
            the 26th Amendment to the United States Con-
            stitution.

1972        July 2. The state legislature established
            a lottery to provide additional revenues
            for the state.

            The state legislature ratified the Equal
            Rights Amendment to the United States Con-
            stitution.

1974        February. National Guard troops were called
            out to patrol the state highways and to pro-
            vide convoy protection for non-striking dri-
            vers during the truckers' strike.

            April 3-4. As a result of terrible tornadoes
            which hit the state, three people were killed.

1975        April 14. Pontiac, Michigan received an All-
            American Cities Award.

            May 21. The Justice Department filed suit in
            the Detroit federal district court which
            charged that Ferndale, a suburb of Detroit,
            was operating a racially segregated school
            system. This was the first suit of this
            type filed by the Justice Department against
            a city and state on behalf of the Office of
            Revenue Sharing.

            July 31. James R. Hoffa was reported missing
            by his family after he failed to return to
            his home in Lake Orion, Michigan.

1976        January 26. Former Governor John B. Swain-
            son received a 60-day prison sentence on
            three counts of perjury. The charge and
            subsequent sentence was based on testimony
            he had given to a federal grand jury
            arising from charges that he had accepted
            a bribe in return for getting a retrial
            for a convicted thief.

            April 1. The state government announced
            its intention to purchase the Ann Arbor
            Railroad.

June 24.  The United States Supreme Court
upheld, 5-4, a Detroit ordinance which
specifically limited the location of
theaters showing films of explicit sexual
activities.

August 14.  President Gerald R. Ford of
Michigan, received the Republican Party's
nomination for President  atthe party's
national convention in Kansas City, Missouri.

November 2.  The residents of the state
voted for a proposition requiring deposits
on beverage containers.  This regulation
was intended as a means of encouraging
recycling and reducing public litter.

1977        August 1.  The AFL-CIO United Steelworkers
Union went on strike in northern Michigan.
T he strike was ended on December 16.

November 18.  The Nuclear Regulatory Commission ordered that a Michigan nuclear
power plant be closed because of possible
safety hazards associated with the electri-
cal connectors.

# BIOGRAPHICAL DIRECTORY

The selected list of governors, United States
Senators and Members of the House of Representatives
for Michigan, 1845-1977, includes all persons listed
in the Chronology for whom basic biographical data was
readily available.  Older biographical sources are
frequently in conflict on certain individuals, and in
such cases the source most commonly cited by later
authorities was preferred.

AITKEN, David Demerest
    Republican
    b. Flint Township, Mich., September 5,
        1853
    d. Flint, Mich., May 26, 1930
    U. S. Representative, 1893-97

ALGER, Russell Alexander
    Republican
    b. Lafayette Township, Ohio, February 27,
        1836
    d. Washington, D. C., January 24, 1907
    Governor of Michigan, 1884-86
    U. S. Secretary of War, 1897-99
    U. S. Senator, 1902-07

ALLEN, Edward Payson
    Republican
    b. Sharon, Mich., October 28, 1852
    d. Ypsilanti, Mich., July 9, 1932
    U. S. Representative, 1896-97

APLIN, Henry Harrison
    Republican
    b. Thetford Township, Mich., April 15, 1841
    d. West Bay City, Mich., July 23, 1910
    U. S. Representative, 1901-03

AVERY, John
    Republican
    b. Watertown, N. Y., February 29, 1824
    d. Greenville, Mich., January 21, 1914
    U. S. Representative, 1893-97

BACON, Mark Reeves
    Republican
    b. Phillipstown, Ill., February 29, 1852
    d. Pasadena, Calif.., August 20, 1941
    U. S. Representative, 1917 -- succeeded by
        Samuel W. Beakes who contested his elec-
        tion.

BALDWIN, Augustus Carpenter
    Union Democrat
    b. Salina (now Syracuse), N. Y., December 24,
        1817
    d. Pontiac, Mich., January 21, 1903
    U. S. Representative, 1863-65

BALDWIN, Henry Porter
    Republican
    b. Coventry, R. I., February 22, 1814
    d. Detroit, Mich., December 31, 1892
    Governor of Michigan, 1869-73
    U. S. Senator, 1879-81

BARRY, John S.
    b. Amherst, N. H., January 29, 1802
    d. Constantine, Mich., January 14, 1870
    Governor of Michigan, 1842-46, 1850-52

BEAKES, Samuel Willard
    Democrat
    b. Burlingham, N. Y., January 11, 1861
    d. Washington, D. C., February 9, 1927
    U. S. Representative, 1913-17, 1917-19

BEAMAN, Fernando Cortez
    Republican
    b. Chester, Vermont, June 28, 1814
    d. Adrian, Mich., September 27, 1882
    U. S. Representative, 1861-71

BEGOLE, Josiah Williams
    Republican
    b. Groveland, N. Y., January 29, 1815
    d. Flint, Mich., June 5, 1896
    U. S. Representative, 1873-75
    Governor of Michigan, 1883-85

BELKNAP. Charles Eugene
    Republican
    b. Massena, N. Y., October 17, 1846
    d. Green Rapids, Mich., January 16, 1929
    U. S. Representative, 1889-91, 1891-93

BENNETT, John Bonifas
    b. Garden, Mich., January 10, 1904
    d. Chevy Chase, Md., August 9, 1964
    U. S. Representative, 1943-45, 1947-64

BENTLEY, Alvin Morell
    Republican
    b. Portland, Maine, August 30, 1918
    d. Tuscon, Ariz., August 10, 1969

BIDDLE, John
    Whig
    b. Philadelphia, Pa., March 2, 1792
    d. White Sulphur Springs, Va., August 25,
        1859
    U. S. Representative (Territorial Delegate),

1829-31

BINGHAM, Kinsley Scott
    Republican
    b. Camillus, N. Y., December 16, 1808
    d. Green Oak, Mich., October 5, 1861
    U. S. Representative, 1847-51
    Governor of Michigan, 1854-58
    U. S. Senator, 1859-61

BISHOP, Roswell Peter
    Republican
    b. Sidney, N. Y., January 6, 1843
    d. Pacific Grove, Calif., March 4, 1920
    U. S. Representative, 1895-1907

BLACKNEY, William Wallace
    Republican
    b. Clio, Mich., August 28, 1876
    d. Flint, Mich., March 14, 1963
    U. S. Representative, 1935-37, 1939-53

BLAIR, Austin
    Republican
    b. Caroline, N. Y., February 8, 1818
    d. Jackson, Mich., August 6, 1894
    Governor of Michigan, 1861-65
    U. S. Representative, 1867-73

BLISS, Aaron Thomas
    Republican
    b. Petersboro, N. Y., May 22, 1837
    d. Milwaukee, Wis., September 16, 1906
    U. S. Representative, 1889-91
    Governor of Michigan,  1901-05

BOHN, Frank Probasco
    Republican
    b. Charlottesville, Ind., July 14, 1866
    d. Newberry, Mich., June 1, 1944
    U. S. Representative, 1927-33

BRADLEY, Edward
    Democrat
    b. East Bloomfield, N. Y., April, 1808
    d. New York, N. Y., August 5, 1847
    U. S. Representative, 1847

BRADLEY, Frederick Van Ness
    Republican
    b. Chicago, Ill., April 12, 1898
    d. New London, Conn., May 24, 1947
    U. S. Representative, 1939-47

BRADLEY, Nathan Ball
    Republican
    b. Lee, Mass., May 28, 1831
    d. Bay City, Mich., November 8, 1906
    U. S. Representative, 1873-77

BREITUNG, Edward
    Republican
    b. in city of Schalkau, Duchy of Saxe-
       Meiningen, Germany, November 10, 1831
    d. Negaunee, Mich., March 3, 1887
    U. S. Representative, 1883-85

BRENNAN, Vincent Morrison
    Republican
    b. Mount Clemens, Mich., April 22, 1890
    d. Detroit, Mich., February 4, 1959
    U. S. Representative, 1921-23

BREWER, Mark Spencer
    Republican
    b. Addison Township, Mich., October 22,
       1837
    d. Washington, D. C., March 18, 1901
    U. S. Representative, 1877-81, 1887-91

BROOMFIELD, William S.
    Republican
    b. Royal Oak, Mich., April 28, 1922
    U. S. Representative, 1957-

BROWN, Garry Eldridge
    Republican
    b. Schoolcraft, Mich., August 12, 1923
    U. S. Representative, 1967-

BROWN, Prentiss Marsh
    Democrat
    b. St. Ignace, Mich., June 18, 1889
    U. S. Representative, 1933-36
    U. S. Senator, 1936-43

BRUCKER, Ferdinand
    Democrat
    b. Bridgeport, Mich., January 8, 1858
    d. Saginaw, Mich., March 3, 1904
    U. S. Representative, 1897-99

BRUCKER, Wilbur M.
    Republican
    b. Saginaw, Mich., June 23, 1894
    Governor of Michigan, 1931-33

BUEL, Alexander Woodruff
    Democrat
    b. Castleton, Vermont, December 13, 1813
    d. Detroit, Mich., April 19, 1868
    U. S. Representative, 1849-51

BURROWS, Julius Caesar
    Republican
    b. North East, Pa., January 9, 1837
    d. Kalamazoo, Mich., November 16, 1915
    U. S. Representative, 1873-75, 1879-83,
        1885-95
    U. S. Senator, 1895-1911

CADY, Claude Ernest
    Democrat
    b. Lansing, Mich., May 28, 1878
    d. Lansing, Mich., November 30, 1953
    U. S. Representative, 1933-35

CARLETON, Ezra Child
    Democrat
    b. St. Clair, Mich., September 6, 1838
    d. Port Huron, Mich., July 24, 1911
    U. S. Representative, 1883-87

CASS, Lewis
    Democrat
    b. Exeter, N. H., October 4, 1782
    d. Detroit, Mich., June 17, 1866
    Governor of Michigan Territory, 1813-31
    U. S. Secretary of War, 1831-36
    U. S. Senator, 1845-48, 1849-57
    U. S. Secretary of War, 1857-60

CEDERBERG, Elford Alfred
    Republican
    b. Bay City, Mich., March 6, 1918
    U. S. Representative, 1953-

CHAMBERLAIN, Charles Ernest
    Republican
    b. Locke Township, Mich., July 22, 1917
    U. S. Representative, 1957-

CHANDLER, Zachariah
    Republican
    b. Bedford, N. H., December 10, 1813
    d. Chicago, Ill., November 1, 1879
    U. S. Senator, 1857-75
    U. S. Secretary of the Interior, 1875-79
    U. S. Senator, 1879

CHIPMAN, John Logan
    Democrat
    b. Detroit, Mich., June 5, 1830
    d. Detroit, Mich., August 17, 1893
    U. S. Representative, 1887-93

CHIPMAN, John Smith
    Democrat
    b. Shoreham, Vermont, August 10, 1800
    d. San Jose, Calif., July 27, 1869
    U. S. Representative, 1845-47

CHRISTIANCY, Isaac Peckham
    Republican
    b. near Johnstown, N. Y., March 12, 1812
    d. Lansing, Mich., September 8, 1890
    U. S. Representative 1875-79

CLANCY, Robert Henry
    Republican
    b. Detroit, Mich., March 14, 1882
    d. Detroit, Mich., April 23, 1962
    U. S. Representative, 1923-25 (Democrat),
        1927-33 (Republican)

CLARDY, Kit Francis
    Republican
    b. Butler, Mo., June 17, 1892
    d. Palos Verdes Estates, Calif., September
        5, 1961
    U. S. Representative, 1953-55

CLARK, Samuel
    Democrat (New York/Michigan)
    b. Clarksville, N. Y., January, 1800
    d. Kalamazoo, Mich., October 2, 1870
    U. S. Representative. 1833-35 (New York),
        1853-55 (Michigan)

CLEVENGER, Ramond Francis
    b. Chicago, Ill., June 6, 1926
    U. S. Representative, 1965-67

CODD, George Pierre
    Republican
    b. Detroit, Mich., December 7, 1869
    d. Detroit Mich., February 16, 1927
    U. S. Representative, 1921-23

COFFIN, Howard Aldridge
    Republican
    b. Middleboro, Mass., June 11, 1877
    d. Washington, D. C., February 28, 1956

U. S. Representative, 1947-49

COMSTOCK, Charles Carter
Fusion Democrat
b. Sullivan, N. H., March 5, 1818
d. Grand Rapids, Mich., February 20, 1900
U. S. Representative, 1885-87

CONGER, James Lockwood
Free-Soil Whig
b. Trenton, N. J., February 18, 1805
d. St. Clair, Mich., April 10, 1876
U. S. Representative, 1851-53

CONGER, Omar Dwight
Republican
b. Cooperstown, N. Y., April 1, 1818
d. Ocean City, Md., July 11, 1898
U. S. Representative, 1869-81
U. S. Senator, 1881-87

CONYERS, John, Jr.
b. Detroit, Mich., May 16, 1929
U. S. Representative, 1965-

COOPER, George Bryan
Democrat
b. Long Hill, N. J., June 6, 1808
d. New Bedford, Wall Township, Mich.,
    August 29, 1866
U. S. Representative, 1859-60

CORLISS, John Blaisdell
Republican
b. Richford, Vermont, June 7, 1851
d. Detroit, Mich., December 24, 1929
U. S. Representative, 1895-1903

COUZENS, James
Republican
b. Chatham, Canada, August 26, 1872
d. Detroit, Mich., October 22, 1936
U. S. Senator, 1922-36

CRAMTON, Louis Convers
Republican
b. Hadley Township, Mich., December 2, 1875
d. Saginaw, Mich., June 23, 1966
U. S. Representative, 1913-31

CRARY, Isaac Edwin
Democrat
b. Preston, Conn., October 2, 1804

d. Marshall, Mich., May 8, 1854
U. S. Representative, 1837-41

CRAWFORD, Fred Lewis
    Republican
    b. Dublin, Texas, May 5, 1888
    d. Washington, D. C., April 13, 1957
    U. S. Representative, 1935-53

CRUMP, Rousseau Owen
    Republican
    b. Pittsford, N. Y., May 20, 1843
    d. West Bay City, Mich., May 1, 1901
    U. S. Representative, 1895-1901

CURRIE, Gilbert Archibald
    Republican
    b. Midland Township, Mich., September 19,
        1882
    d. Midland, Mich., June 5, 1960
    U. S. Representative, 1917-21

CUTCHEON, Bryan M.
    Republican
    b. Pembroke, N. H., May 11, 1836
    d. Ypsilanti, Mich., April 12, 1908
    U. S. Representative, 1883-91

DARRAGH, Archibald Bard
    Republican
    b. La Salle Township, Mich, December 23,
        1840
    d. St. Louis, Mich., February 21, 1927
    U. S. Representative, 1901-09

DENBY, Edwin
    Republican
    b. Evansville, Ind., February 18, 1870
    d. Detroit, Mich., February 8, 1929
    U. S. Representative, 1905-11
    U. S. Secretary of the Navy, 1921-24

DICKINSON, Luren D.
    Republican
    Governor of Michigan, 1939-41

DIEKEMA, Geritt John
    Republican
    b. Holland, Mich., March 27, 1859
    d. The Hague, Netherlands
    U. S. Representative, 1908-11
    U. S. Minister to the Netherlands, 1929-30

DIGGS, Charles Coles, Jr.
    Democrat
    b. Detroit, Mich., December 2, 1922
    U. S. Representative, 1955-

DINGELL, John David
    Democrat
    b. Detroit, Mich., February 2, 1894
    d. Washington, D. C., September 19, 1955
    U. S. Representative, 1933-55

DINGELL, John David, Jr.
    Democrat
    b. Colorado Springs, Colo., July 8, 1926
    U. S. Representative, 1955

DODDS, Francis Henry
    Republican
    b. Waddington, N. Y., June 9, 1858
    d. Mt. Pleasant, Mich., December 23, 1940
    U. S. Representative, 1909-13

DOREMUS, Frank Ellsworth
    Democrat
    b. Venango County, Pa., August 31, 1865
    d.Howell, Mich., September 4, 1947
    U.S. Representative, 1911-21

DRIGGS, John Fletcher
    Republican
    b. Kinderhook, N. Y., March 8, 1813
    d. East Saginaw, Mich., December 17, 1877
    U. S. Representative, 1863-69

DURAND, George Harman
    Democrat
    b. Cobleskill, N. Y., February 21, 1838
    d. Flint, Mich., June 8, 1903
    U. S. Representative, 1875-77

ELDREDGE, Nathaniel Buel
    b. Auburn, N. Y., March 28, 1813
    d. Adrian, Mich., November 27, 1893
    U. S. Representative, 1883-87

ELLSWORTH, Charles Clinton
    Republican
    b. West Berkshire, Vermont, January 29,
        1824
    d. Greenville, Mich., June 25, 1899
    U. S. Representative, 1877-79

ENGEL, Albert Joseph
    Republican
    b. New Washington, Ohio, January 1, 1888
    d. Grand Rapids, Mich., December 2, 1959
    U. S. Representative, 1935-51

ESCH, Marvin L.
    Republican
    b. Flinton, Pa., August 4, 1927
    U. S. Representative, 1967-

FARNUM, Billie Sunday
    Democrat
    b. Saginaw, Mich., April 11, 1916
    U. S. Representative, 1965-67

FELCH, Alpheus
    Democrat
    b. Limerick, Maine, September 28, 1804
    d. Ann Arbor, Mich., June 13, 1896
    Governor of Michigan, 1846-47
    U. S. Senator, 1847-53

FERGUSON, Homer
    Republican
    b. Harrison City, Pa., February 25, 1889
    U. S. Senator, 1943-55

FERRIS, Woodbridge Nathan
    Democrat
    b. Spencer, N. Y., January 6, 1853
    d. Washington, D. C., March 23, 1928
    Governor of Michigan, 1913-17
    U. S. Senator, 1923-28

FERRY, Thomas White
    Republican
    b. Mackinac Island, Mich., June 10, 1827
    d. Grand Haven, Mich., October 13, 1896
    U. S. Representative, 1865-71
    U. S. Senator, 1871-83, President pro tem-
        pore, 1875-79

FIELD, Moses Whelock
    Republican
    b. Watertown, N. Y., February 10, 1828
    d. Hamtramck (suburb of Detroit), Mich.,
        March 14, 1889
    U. S. Representative, 1873-75

FISHER, Spencer Oliver
    Democrat

b. Camden, Mich., February 3, 1843
d. Bay City, Mich., June 1, 1919
U. S. Representative, 1885-89

FITZGERALD, Frank D.
Republican
b. Grand Ledge, Mich., January 27, 1885
d. March 16, 1939
Governor of Michigan, 1935-37, 1939

FITZGERALD, Thomas
Democrat
b. Germantown, N. Y., April 10, 1796
d. Niles, Mich., March 25, 1855
U. S. Senator, 1848-49

FORD, Gerald R., Jr.
Republican
b. Omaha, Nebraska, July 14, 1913
U. S. Representative, 1949-73
Vice President of the United States, 1973-74
President of the United States, 1974-77

FORD, Melbourne Haddock
Democrat
b. Salem, Mich., June 30, 1849
d. Grand Michigan, April 20, 1891
U. S. Representative, 1887-89, 1891

FORD, William David
Democrat
b. Herkimer County, N. Y., August 6, 1927
U. S. Representative, 1965-

FORDNEY, Joseph Warren
Republican
b. Hartford City, Ind., November 5, 1853
d. Saginaw, Mich., January 8, 1932
U. S. Representative, 1899-23

FOSTER, Wilder De Ayr
Republican
b. Orange County, N. Y., January 8, 1819
d. Grand Rapids, Mich., September 20, 1873
U. S. Representative, 1871-73

FOULKES, George Ernest
Democrat
b. Chicago, Ill., December 25, 1878
d. Hartford, Mich., December 13, 1960
U. S. Representative, 1933-35

FRANKHAUSER, William Horace
Republican

b. Wood County, Ohio, March 5, 1863
d. Battle Creek, Mich., May 9, 1921
U. S. Representative, 1921

GARDNER, Washington
   Republican
   b. Morrow County, Ohio, February 16, 1845
   d. Albion, Mich., March 31, 1928
   U. S. Representative, 1899-1911

GORDON, James W.
   Whig
   Governor of Michigan, 1841-42

GORMAN, James Sedgwick
   Democrat
   b. Lyndon Township, Mich., December 28,
      1850
   d. Detroit, Mich., May 27, 1923
   U. S. Representative, 1891-95

GRANGER, Bradley Francis
   Democrat
   b. Suffield, Conn., March 12, 1825
   d. Syracuse, N. Y., November 4, 1882
   U. S. Representative, 1861-63

GREEN, Fred W.
   b. Manister, Mich., October 20, 1872
   d. November 30, 1936
   Governor of Michigan, 1927-31

GREENLY, William L.
   DEMOCRAT
   Governor of Michigan, 1847-48

GRIFFIN, Levi Thomas
   Democrat
   b. Clinton, N. Y., May 23, 1837
   d. Detroit, Mich., March 17, 1906
   U. S. Representative, 1893-95

GRIFFIN, Robert Paul
   b. Detroit, Mich., November 6, 1923
   U. S. Representative, 1957-66
   U. S. Senator, 1966-

GRIFFITHS, Martha Wright
   Democrat
   b. Pierce City, Mo., January 29, 1912
   U. S. Representative, 1955-

GROESBECK, Alex J.
    Republican
    b. Warren, Mich., November 7, 1873
    d. March 10, 1953
    Governor of Michigan, 1921-27

HAMILTON, Edward La Rue
    Republican
    b. Niles Township, Mich., December 9, 1857
    d. St. Joseph, Mich., November 2, 1923
    U. S. Representative, 1897-1921

HART, Michael James
    Democrat
    b. Waterloo, Canada, July 16, 1877
    d. Saginaw, Mich., February 14, 1951
    U. S. Representative, 1931-35

HART, Philip A.
    Democrat
    b. Bryn Mawr, Pa., December 10, 1912
    U. S. Senator, 1959-

HARVEY, James
    Republican
    b. Iron Mountain, Mich., July 4, 1922
    U. S. Representative, 1961-

HATCH, Herschel Harrison
    Republican
    b. Morrisville, N. Y., February 17, 1837
    d. Detroit, Mich., November 30, 1920
    U. S. Representative, 1883-85

HAYWORTH, Donald
    Democrat
    b. Toledo, Iowa, January 13, 1898
    U. S. Representative, 1955-57

HOFFMAN, Clare Eugene
    Republican
    b. Vicksburg, Pa., September 10, 1875
    d. Allegan, Mich., November 3, 1867
    U. S. Representative, 1935-63

HOOK, Frank Eugene
    Democrat
    b. L'Anse, Mich., May 26, 1893
    U. S. Representative, 1935-43, 1945-47

HOOPER, Joseph Lawrence
    Republican
    b. Cleveland, Ohio, December 22, 1877

d. Washington, D. C., February 22, 1934
U. S. Representative, 1925-34

HORR, Roswell, Gilbert
    Republican
    b. Waitsfield, Vermont, November 26, 1830
    d. Plainfield, N. J., December 19, 1896
    U. S. Representative, 1879-85

HOUSEMAN, Julius
    Democrat
    b. Zeckendorf, Bavaria, Germany, December
        8, 1832
    d. Grand Rapids, Mich., February 8, 1891
    U. S. Representative, 1883-85

HOWARD, Jacob Merritt
    Republican
    b. Shaftsbury, Vermont, July 10, 1805
    d. Detroit, Mich., April 2, 1871
    U. S. Representative, 1841-43 (Whig)
    U. S. Senator, 1862-71 (Republican)

HOWARD, William Alanson
    Republican
    b. Hinesburg, Vermont, April 8, 1813
    d. Washington, D. C., April 10, 1880
    U. S. Representative, 1855-59, 1860-61
    Governor of Dakota Territory, 1878-80

HUBBELL, Jay Abel
    Republican
    b. Avon, Mich., September 15, 1829
    d. Bellville, Ohio, October 13, 1900
    U. S. Representative, 1873-83

HUDSON, Grant Martin
    Republican
    b. Eaton Township, Ohio, July 23, 1868
    d. Kalamazoo, Mich., October 26, 1955
    U. S. Representative, 1923-31

HUNT, James Bennett
    Democrat
    b. Demerara, British Guiana, South America,
        August 13, 1799
    d. Washington, D. C., August 15, 1857
    U. S. Representative, 1843-47

HUTCHINSON, Edward
    Republican
    b. Fennville, Mich., October 13, 1914
    U. S. Representative, 1963-

JAMES, William Francis (Frank)
    Republican
    b. Morristown, N. J., May 23, 1873
    d. Arlington, Va., November 17, 1945
    U. S. Representative, 1915-35

JEROME, David H.
    Republican
    Governor of Michigan, 1881-83

JONES, George Wallace
    ---- (Michigan/Wisconsin/Iowa)
    b. Vincennes, Ind., April 12, 1804
    d. Dubuque, Iowa, July 22, 1896
    U. S. Representative (Territorial Delegate),
        1835-36 (Michigan), 1836-39 (Wisconsin)
    U. S. Senator, 1848-59 (Iowa)

JONKMAN, Bartel John
    Republican
    b. Grand Rapids, Mich., April 28, 1884
    d. Grand Rapids, Mich., June 13, 1955
    U. S. Representative, 1940-49

KEIGHTLEY, Edwin William
    Republican
    b. near Scott, Ind., August 7, 1843
    d. Constantine, Mich., May 4, 1926
    U. S. Representative, 1877-79

KELLEY, Patrick Henry
    Republican
    b. near Dowagiac, Silver Creek Township,
        Mich., October 7, 1867
    d. Washington, D. C., September 11, 1925
    U. S. Representative, 1913-23

KELLOGG, Francis William
    Republican (Michigan/Alabama)
    b. Worthington, Mass., May 30, 1810
    d. Alliance, Ohio, January 13, 1879
    U. S. Representative, 1859-65 (Michigan),
        1868-69 (Alabama)

KELLY, Harry F.
    Republican
    Governor of Michigan, 1943-47

KETCHAM, John Clark
    Republican
    b. Toledo, Ohio, January 1, 1873
    d. Hastings, Mich., December 4, 1941
    U. S. Representative, 1921-33

KIMBALL, Henry Mahlon
    Republican
    b. Orland, Ind., August 27, 1878
    d. Kalamazoo, Mich., October 19, 1935
    U. S. Representative, 1935

KNOX, Victor Alfred
    Republican
    b. on farm, Chippewa County, Mich., January
        13, 1899
    U. S. Representative, 1953-65

LACEY, Edward Samuel
    Republican
    b. Chili, N. Y., November 26, 1835
    d. Evanston, Ill., October 2, 1916
    U. S. Representative, 1881-85

LEACH, DeWitt Clinton
    Republican
    b. Clarence, N. Y., November 23, 1822
    d. Springfield, Mo., December 21, 1909
    U. S. Representative, 1857-61

LEHR, John Camillus
    Democrat
    b. Monroe, Mich., November 18, 1878
    d. Monroe, Mich., February 17, 1958
    U. S. Representative, 1933-35

LESINSKI, John
    Democrat
    b. Erie, Pa., January 3, 1885
    d. Detroit, Mich., May 27, 1950
    U. S. Representative, 1933-50

LESINSKI, John, Jr.
    Democrat
    b. Detroit, Mich., December 28, 1914
    U. S. Representative, 1951-65

LINDQUIST, Francis Oscar
    Republican
    b. Marinette, Wis., September 27, 1869
    d. Grand Rapids, Mich., September 25,
        1924
    U. S. Representative, 1913-15

LINTON, William Seelye
    Republican
    b. St. Clair, Mich., February 4, 1856
    d. Lansing, Mich., November 22, 1927
    U. S. Representative, 1893-97

LONGYEAR, John Wesley
    Republican
    b. Shandaken, N. Y., October 22, 1820
    d. Detroit, Mich., March 11, 1875
    U. S. Representative, 1863-67

LORD, Henry William
    Republican
    b. Northampton, Mass., March 8, 1821
    d. in railroad accident near Butte, Mont.,
        January 25, 1891
    U. S. Representative, 1881-83

LOUD, George Alvin
    Republican
    b. Bracebridge, Ohio, June 18, 1852
    d. in automobile accident, Myrtle Point,
        Mich., November 13, 1925
    U. S. Representative, 1903-13, 1915-17

LUCE, Cyrus G.
    Republican
    b. Windsor, Ohio, July 2, 1824
    d. Coldwater, Mich., 1905
    Governor of Michigan, 1887-91

LUCKING, Alfred
    Democrat
    b. Ingersoll, Ontario, Canada, December 8,
        1856
    d. Detroit, Mich., December 1, 1929
    U. S. Representative, 1903-05

LUECKE, John Frederick
    Democrat
    b. Escanaba, Mich., July 4, 1889
    d. Escanaba, Mich., March 21, 1952
    U. S. Representative, 1937-39

LYON, Lucius
    Democrat
    b. Shelburne, Vermont, February 26, 1800
    d. Detroit, Mich., September 24, 1851
    U. S. Representative (Territorial Delegate),
        1833-35, Representative, 1843-45
    U. S. Senator, 1837-39

MACDONALD, William Josiah
    Progressive
    b. Potosi, Wis., November 17, 1873
    d. Chicago, Ill., March 29, 1946
    U. S. Representative, 1913-15

MACHROWICZ, Thaddeus Michael
    Democrat
    b. Gostyn, Poland, August 21, 1899
    d. Bloomfield Township, February 17, 1970
    U. S. Representative, 1951-61

MACKIE, John C.
    Democrat
    b. Toronto, Province of Ontario, Canada,
        June 1, 1920
    U. S. Representative, 1965-67

MAIN, Verner Wright
    Republican
    b. Ashley, Ohio, December 16, 1885
    d. Battle Creek, Mich., July 6, 1965
    U. S. Representative, 1935-37

MAPES, Carl Edgar
    Republican
    b. near Kalamazoo, Mich., December 26, 1874
    d. New Orleans, La., December 12, 1939
    U. S. Representative, 1913-39

MASON, Stevens T.
    Democrat
    b. Loudon County, Va., October 27, 1811
    d. January 4, 1843
    Governor of Michigan, 1837-40

MCCLELLAND, Robert
    Democrat
    b. Greencastle, Pa., August 1, 1807
    d. Detroit, Mich., August 30, 1880
    U. S. Representative, 1843-49
    Governor of Michigan, 1851-53
    U. S. Secretary of the Interior, 1853-57

MCDONALD, Jack H.
    Republican
    b. Detroit, Mich., June 28, 1932
    U. S. Representative, 1967-

MCGOWAN, Jonas Hurtzell
    Republican
    b. Township of Smithtown, Ohio, April 2,
        1837
    d. Washington, D. C., July 5, 1909
    U. S. Representative, 1877-81

MCINTOSH, Robert John
    Republican
    b. Port Huron, Mich., September 16, 1922

U. S. Representative, 1957-59

MCLAUGHLIN, James Campbell
    Republican
    b. Beardstown, Ill., January 26, 1858
    d. Marion, Va., while en route to Washing-
        ton, D. C., November 29, 1932
    U. S. Representative, 1907-32

MCLEOD, Clarence John
    Republican
    b. Detroit, Mich., July 3, 1895
    d. Detroit, Mich., May 15, 1954
    U. S. Representative, 1920-21, 1923-37,
        1939-41

MCMILLAN, James
    Republican
    b. Hamilton, Ontario, May 12, 1838
    d. Manchester, Mass., August 10, 1902
    U. S. Senator, 1889-1902

MCMORRAN, Henry Gordon
    Republican
    b. Port Huron, Mich., June 11, 1844
    d. Port Huron, Mich., July 19, 1929
    U. S. Representative, 1903-13

MCNAMARA, Patrick Vincent
    Democrat
    b. North Weymouth, Mass., October 4, 1894
    d. Bethesda, Md., April 30, 1966
    U. S. Senator, 1955-66

MEADER, George
    Republican
    b. Benton Harbor, Mich., September 13,
        1907
    U. S. Representative, 1951-65

MESICK, William
    Republican
    b. Neward, N. Y., August 26, 1856
    d. Petoskey, Mich., December 1, 1942
    U. S. Representative, 1897-1901

MICHENER, Earl Cory
    Republican
    b. near Attica, Ohio, November 30, 1876
    d. Adrian, Mich., July 4, 1957
    U. S. Representative, 1919-33, 1935-51

MILLIKEN, William G.
    Republican
    b. Traverse City, Mich., March 26, 1922
    Governor of Michigan, 1969-

MILNES, Alfred
    Republican
    b. Bradford, Yorkshire, England, May 28,
        1844
    d. Coldwater, Mich., January 15, 1916
    U. S. Representative, 1895-97

MOFFATT, Seth Crittenden
    Republican
    b. Battle Creek, Mich., August 10, 1841
    d. Washington, D. C., December 22, 1887
    U. S. Representative, 1885-87

MOODY, Arthur Edson Blair
    Democrat
    b. New Haven, Conn., February 13, 1902
    d. Ann Arbor, Mich., July 20, 1954
    U. S. Senator, 1951-52

MOOR, John Wesley
    Republican
    b. near Ypsilanti, Mich., January 18, 1836
    d. Muskegan, Mich., April 5, 1898
    U. S. Representative, 1893-95

MURPHY, Frank
    Democrat
    b. Harbor Beach, Mich., April 13, 1890
    d. July 19, 1949
    Governor of Michigan, 1937-39

MUSSELWHITE, Harry Webster
    Democrat
    b. near Coldwater, Mich., May 23, 1868
    d. San Lorenzo, Calif., December 14, 1955
    U. S. Representative, 1933-35

NEDZI, Lucien Norbert
    Democrat
    b. Hamtramck, Mich., May 28, 1925
    U. S. Representative, 1961-

NEWBERRY, John Stoughton
    Republican
    b. Waterville, N. Y., November 18, 1826
    d. Detroit, Mich., January 2, 1887
    U. S. Representative, 1879-81

NEWBERRY, Truman Handy
    Republican
    b. Detroit, Mich., November 5, 1864
    d. Grosse Pointe, Mich., October 3, 1945
    U. S. Secretary of the Navy, 1908-09
    U. S. Senator, 1919-22

NICHOLS, Charles Archibald
    Republican
    b. Boyne City, Mich., August 25, 1876
    d. Washington, D. C., April 25, 1920
    U. S. Representative, 1915-20

NOBLE, David Addison
    Democrat
    b. Williamstown, Mass., November 9, 1802
    d. Monroe, Mich., October 13, 1876
    U. S. Representative, 1853-55

NORVELL, John
    Democrat
    b. Danville, Va. (now Kentucky), December
       21, 1789
    d. Detroit, Mich., April 24, 1850
    U. S. Senator, 1837-41

OAKMEER, Charles Gibb
    Republican
    b. Detroit, Mich., September 4, 1903
    U. S. Representative, 1933-55

O'BRIEN, George Donoghue
    Democrat
    b. Detroit, Mich., January 1, 1900
    d. Washington, D. C., October 25, 1957
    U. S. Representative, 1937-39, 1941-47,
      1949-55

O'DONNELL, James
    Republican
    b. Norwalk, Conn., March 25, 1840
    d. Jackson, Mich., March 17, 1915
    U. S. Representative, 1885-93

O'HARA, James Grant
    Democrat
    b. Washington, D. C., November 8, 1925
    U. S. Representative, 1959-

OSBORNE, Charles S.
    Republican
    Governor of Michigan, 1911-13

PALMER, Thomas Witherell
    Republican
    b. Detroit, Mich., January 25, 1830
    d. Detroit, Mich., June 1, 1913
    U. S. Senator, 1883-89

PARSONS, Andrew
    Democrat
    Governor of Michigan, 1853-55

PATTON, John, Jr.
    Republican
    b. Curwensville, Pa., October 30, 1850
    d. Grand Rapids, Mich., May 24, 1907
    U. S. Senator, 1894-95

PECK, George Washington
    Democrat
    b. New York, N. Y., June 4, 1818
    d. Saginaw, Mich., June 30, 1905
    U. S. Representative, 1855-57

PENNIMAN, Ebenezer Jenckes
    Whig/Free Soiler
    b. Lansingburgh, N. Y., January 11, 1804
    d. Plymouth, Mich., April 12, 1890
    U. S. Representative, 1851-53

PERSON, Seymour Howe
    Republican
    b. near Howell, Howell Township, Mich.,
        February 2, 1879
    d. Lansing, Mich., April 7, 1957
    U. S. Representative, 1931-33

PINGREE, Hazen S.
    Republican
    b. Denmark, Maine, August 30, 1840
    d. Detroit, Mich., 1901
    Governor of Michigan, 1897-1901

PORTER, Augustus Seymour
    Whig
    b. Canandaigua, N. Y., January 18, 1798
    d. Niagara Falls, N. Y., September 18,
        1872
    U. S. Representative, 1840-45

POTTER, Allen
    Independent
    b. Galloway, N. Y., October 2, 1818
    d. Kalamazoo, Mich., May 8, 1885
    U. S. Representative, 1875-77

POTTER, Charles Edward
    Republican
    b. Lapeer, Mich., October 30, 1916
    U. S. Representative, 1947-52
    U. S. Senator, 1952-59

RABAUT, Louis Charles
    Democrat
    b. Detroit, Mich., December 5, 1886
    d. Hamtramck, Mich., November 12, 1961
    U. S. Representative, 1935-47, 1949-61

RANSOM, Epaphroditus
    Democrat
    Governor of Michigan, 1848-50

RICH, John Tyler
    Republican
    b. Conneautville, Pa., April 23, 1841
    d. St. Petersburg, Florida, March 28,
        1926
    U. S. Representative, 1881-83
    Governor of Michigan, 1892-96

RICHARD, Gabriel
    ----
    b. La Ville de Saintes, France, October 15,
        1767
    d. Detroit, Mich., September 13, 1832
    U. S. Representative (Territorial Delegate),
        1823-25

RICHARDSON, George Frederick
    Democrat
    b. Jamestown, Mich., July 1, 1850
    d. Bellevue, Wash., March 1, 1923
    U. S. Representative, 1893-95

RIEGLE, Donald Wayne, Jr.
    Republican
    b. Flint, Mich., February 4, 1938
    U. S. Representative, 1967-

ROMNEY, George W.
    Republican
    b. Chihuahua, Mexico, July 8, 1907
    Governor of Michigan, 1963-69
    U. S. Secretary of Housing and Urban De-
        velopment, 1969-72

RUPPE, Philip E.
    Republican
    b. Laurium, Mich., September 29, 1926

U. S. Representative, 1967-

RYAN, Harold Martin
    Democrat
    b. Detroit, Mich., February 6, 1911
    U. S. Representative, 1962-65

SADOWSKI, George Gregory
    Democrat
    b. Detroit, Mich., March 12, 1903
    d. Utica, Mich., October 9, 1961
    U. S. Representative, 1933-39, 1939-51

SCOTT, Frank Douglas
    Republican
    b. Alpena, Mich., August 25, 1878
    d. Palm Beach, Florida, February 12, 1951
    U. S. Representative, 1915-27

SEYMOUR, Henry William
    Republican
    b. Brockport, N. Y., July 21, 1834
    d. Washington, D. C., April 7, 1906
    U. S. Representative, 1888-89

SHAFER, Paul Werntz
    Republican
    b. Elkhart, Ind., April 27, 1893
    d. Washington, D. C., August 17, 1954
    U. S. Representative, 1937-54

SHELDEN, Carlos Douglas
    Republican
    b. Walworth, Wis., June 10, 1840
    d. Houghton, Mich., June 29, 1904
    U. S. Representative, 1897-1903

SIBLEY, Solomon
    ----
    b. Sutton, Mass., October 7, 1769
    d. Detroit, Mich., April 4, 1846
    U. S. Representative (Territorial Delegate),
    1820-23

SIGLER, Kim
    Republican
    Governor of Michigan, 1947-49

SLEEPER, Albert E.
    Republican
    b. Bradford, Vermont
    d. Bad Axe, Mich., May 13, 1934
    Governor of Michigan, 1917-21

SMITH, Henry Cassorte
    Republican
    b. Canandaigua, N. Y., June 2, 1856
    d. Adrian, Mich., December 7, 1911
    U. S. Representative, 1899-1903

SMITH, John M. C.
    Republican
    b. Belfast, Ireland, February 6, 1853
    d. Charlotte, Mich., March 30, 1923
    U. S. Representative, 1911-21, 1921-23

SMITH, Samuel William
    Republican
    b. Independence Township, Mich., August
        23, 1852
    d. Detroit, Mich., June 19, 1931
    U. S. Representative, 1897-1915

SMITH, William
    Republican
    b. Dowagiac, Mich., May 12, 1859
    d. Grand Rapids, Mich., October 11, 1932
    U. S. Representative, 1895-1907
    U. S. Senator, 1907-19

SNOVER, Horace Greeley
    Republican
    b. Romeo, Mich., September 21, 1847
    d. Port Huron, Mich., July 21, 1824
    U. S. Representative, 1895-99

SOSNOWSKI, John Bartholomew
    Republican
    b. Detroit, Mich., December 8, 1883
    d. Detroit, Mich., July 16, 1968
    U. S. Representative, 1925-27

SPALDING, George
    Republican
    b. Blaisgowrie, Perthshire, Scotland, No-
        vember 12, 1836
    d. Monroe, Mich., September 13, 1915
    U. S. Representative, 1895-99

SPAULDING, Oliver Lyman
    Republican
    b. Jaffrey, N. H., August 2, 1833
    d. Washington, D. C., July 30, 1922
    U. S. Representative, 1881-83

SPRAGUE, William
    Whig

b. Providence, R. I., February 23, 1809
d. Kalamazoo, Mich., September 19, 1868
U. S. Representative, 1849-51

STOEBLER, Neil Oliver
Democrat
b. Ann Arbor, Mich., July 11, 1905
U. S. Representative, 1963-65

STEPHENSON, Samuel Merritt
Republican
b. Hartland, New Brunswick, Canada, December
23, 1831
d. Menominee, Mich., July 31, 1907
U. S. Representative, 1889-97

STEVENS, Hester Lockhart
Democrat
b. Lima, N. Y., October 1, 1803
d. Georgetown, D. C., May 7, 1864
U. S. Representative, 1853-55

STOCKBRIDGE, Francis Brown
Republican
b. Bath, Maine, April 9, 1826
d. Chicago, Ill., April 30, 1894
U. S. Senator, 1887-94

STONE, John Wesley
Republican
b. Wadsworth, Ohio, July 18, 1838
d. Lansing, Mich., March 24, 1922
U. S. Representative, 1877-81

STOUGHTON, William Lewis
Republican
b. Bangor, N. Y., March 20, 1827
d. Sturgis, Mich., June 6, 1888
U. S. Representative, 1869-73

STOUT, Byron Gray
Democrat
b. Richmond, N. Y., January 12, 1829
d. Pontiac, Mich., June 19, 1896
U. S. Representative, 1891-93

STRICKLAND, Randolph
Republican
b. Dansville, N. Y., February 4, 1823
d. Battle Creek, Mich., May 5, 1880
U. S. Representative, 1869-71

STUART, Charles Edward
    Democrat
    b. near Waterloo, N. Y., November 25, 1810
    d. Kalamazoo, Mich., May 19, 1887
    U. S. Representative, 1847-49, 1851-53
    U. S. Senator, 1853-59

STUART, David Rice
    Democrat
    b. Brooklyn, N. Y., March 12, 1816
    d. Detroit, Mich., September 12, 1868
    U. S. Representative, 1853-55

SUTHERLAND, Jabez Gridley
    Democrat
    b. Van Buren, N. Y., October 6, 1825
    d. Berkeley, Calif., November 20, 1902
    U. S. Representative, 1871-73

SWAINSON, John B.
    Democrat
    b. 1924
    Governor of Michigan, 1961-63

SWEET, Edwin Forrest
    Democrat
    b. Dansville, N. Y., November 21, 1847
    d. Ojai, Calif., April 2, 1935
    U. S. Representative, 1911-13

TARSNEY, Timothy Edward
    Democrat
    b. Medina, Mich., February 4, 1849
    d. Kansas City, Mo., June 8, 1909
    U. S. Representative, 1885-89

TENEROWICZ, Rudolph Gabriel
    Democrat
    b. Budapest, Austria, June 14, 1890
    d. Hamtramck, Mich., August 31, 1963
    U. S. Representative, 1939-43

THOMAS, Henry Franklin
    Republican
    b. Tompkins, Mich., December 17, 1843
    d. Allegan, Mich., April 16, 1912
    U. S. Representative, 1893-97

THOMPSON, Ruth
    Republican
    b. Whitehall, Mich., September 15, 1887
    d. Plainwell Sanitorium, Allegan County,
        Mich., April 5, 1970

U. S. Representative, 1951-57

TODD, Albert May
    Fusionist
    b. Nottawa, Mich., June 3, 1850
    d. Kalamazoo, Mich., October 6, 1931
    U. S. Representative, 1897-99

TODD, Paul H., Jr.
    Democrat
    b. Kalamazoo, Mich., September 22, 1921
    U. S. Representative, 1965-67

TOWNSEND, Charles Elroy
    Republican
    b. near Concord, Mich., August 15, 1856
    d. Jackson, Mich., August 3, 1924
    U. S. Representative, 1903-11
    U. S. Senator, 1911-23

TRANSUE, Andrew Jackson
    Democrat
    b. Clarksville, Mich., January 12, 1903
    U. S. Representative, 1837-39

TROWBRIDGE, Rowland Ebenezer
    Republican
    b. Horseheads, N. Y., June 18, 1821
    d. Birmingham, Mich., April 20, 1881
    U. S. Representative, 1861-63, 1865-69

UPSON, Charles
    Republican
    b. Southington, Conn., March 19, 1821
    d. Coldwater, Mich., September 5, 1885
    U. S. Representative, 1863-69

VANDENBERG, Arthur Hendrick
    Republican
    b. Grand Rapids, Mich., March 22, 1884
    d. Grand Rapids, Mich., April 18, 1951
    U. S. Senator, 1928-51, President pro tem-
        pore, 1947-49

VANDER JAGT, Guy Adrian
    Republican
    b. Cadillac, Mich., August 26, 1931
    U. S. Representative, 1966-

VAN WAGONER, Murray D.
    Democrat
    Governor of Michigan, 1941-43

VINCENT, Bird J.
    Republican
    b. near Clarkston, Mich., March 6, 1880
    d. on board the transport <u>Henderson</u> while
       en route to the U. S. from Honolulu,
       Hawaii, July 18, 1931
    U. S. Representative, 1923-31

VIVIAN, Weston Edward
    Democrat
    b. Newfoundland, Canada, October 25, 1924
    U. S. Representative, 1965-67

WALBRIDGE, David Safford
    Republican
    b. Bennington, Vermont, July 30, 1802
    d. Kalamazoo, Mich., June 15, 1868
    U. S. Representative, 1855-59

WALDRON, Henry
    Republican
    b. Albany, N. Y., October 11, 1819
    d. Hillsdale, Mich., September 13, 1868
    U. S. Representative, 1855-59

WEADCOCK, Thomas Addis Emmet
    Democrat
    b. Ballygarrett, Ireland, January 1, 1850
    d. Detroit, Mich., November 18, 1938
    U. S. Representative, 1891-95

WEBBER, George Washington
    Republican
    b. Newbury, Vermont, November 25, 1825
    d. Ionia, Mich., January 15, 1900
    U. S. Representative, 1881-83

WEDEMEYER, William Walter
    Republican
    b. near Lima Township, Mich., March 22,
       1873
    d. while on an official visit to Colon,
       Panama, January 2, 1913
    U. S. Representative, 1911-13

WEEKS, Edgar
    Republican
    b. Mount Clemens, Mich., August 3, 1839
    d. Mount Clemens, Mich., December 17, 1904
    U. S. Representative, 1899-1903

WEIDEMAN, Carl May
    Democrat

b. Detroit, Mich., March 5, 1898
U. S. Representative, 1933-35

WHEELER, Frank Willis
    Republican
    b. Chaumont, N. Y., March 2, 1853
    d. Saginaw, Mich., August 9, 1921
    U. S. Representative, 1889-91

WHEELER, Harrison H.
    Democrat
    b. Farmers Creek, Mich., March 22, 1839
    d. Farmers Creek, Mich., July 28, 1896
    U. S. Representative, 1891-93

WHITING, Justin Rice
    Democrat - Greenbacker
    b. Bath, N. Y., February 18, 1897
    d. St. Clair, Mich., January 31, 1903
    U. S. Representative, 1887-95

WILLARD, George
    Republican
    b. Bolton, Vermont, March 20, 1824
    d. Battle Creek, Mich., March 26, 1901
    U. S. Representative, 1873-77

WILLIAMS, Alpheus Starkey
    Democrat
    b. Saybrook, Conn., September 20, 1810
    d. Washington, D. C., December 20, 1878
    U. S. Representative, 1875-78

WILLIAMS, Arthur Bruce
    Republican
    b. Ashland, Ohio, January 27, 1872
    d. Baltimore, Md., May 1, 1925
    U. S. Representative, 1923-25

WILLIAMS, G. Mennen
    Democrat
    b. Detroit, Mich., February 23, 1911
    Governor of Michigan, 1949-61
    Justice of Michigan Supreme Court, 1971-

WILLIAMS, William Brewster
    Republican
    b. Pittsford, N. Y., July 28, 1826
    d. Allegan, Mich., March 4, 1905
    U. S. Representative, 1873-77

WILLITS, Edwin
    Republican
    b. Otto, N. Y., April 24, 1830
    d. Washington, D. C., October 22, 1896
    U. S. Representative, 1877-83

WINANS, Edwin Baruch
    Democrat
    b. Avon, N. Y., May 16, 1826
    d. Hamburg, Mich., July 4, 1894
    U. S. Representative, 1883-87
    Governor of Michigan, 1891-93

WING, Austin Elia
    Whig
    b. Conway, Mass., February 3, 1792
    d. Cleveland, Ohio, August 27, 1849
    U. S. Representative (Territorial Delegate),
        1825-29, 1831-33

WISNER, Moses
    Republican
    Governor of Michigan, 1859-61

WOLCOTT, Jesse Paine
    Republican
    b. Gardner, Mass., March 3, 1893
    d. Chevy Chase, Md., January 28, 1968
    U. S. Representative, 1931-57

WOODBRIDGE, William W.
    Whig - Democrat
    b. Norwich, Conn., August 20, 1780
    d. Detroit, Mich., October 20, 1861
    U. S. Representative (Territorial Delegate),
        1819-20
    Governor of Michigan, 1840-41
    U. S. Senator, 1841-47

WOODRUFF, Roy Orchard
    Republican
    b. Eaton Rapids, Mich., March 14, 1876
    d. Washington, D. C., February 12, 1953
    U. S. Representative, 1913-15 (Progressive
        Republican), 1921-53 (Republican)

YAPLE, George Lewis
    Unionist
    b. Leonidas, Mich., February 20, 1851
    d. Mendon, Mich., December 16, 1939
    U. S. Representative, 1883-85

YOUMANS, Henry Melville
    Democrat
    b. Otego, N. Y., May 15, 1832
    d. Saginaw, Mich., July 8, 1920
    U. S. Representative, 1891-93

YOUNG, Horace Olin
    Republican
    b. New Albion, N. Y., August 4, 1850
    d. Ishpeming, Mich., August 5, 1917
    U. S. Representative, 1903-13

YOUNGBLOOD, Harold Francis
    Republican
    b. Detroit, Mich., August 7, 1907
    U. S. Representative, 1947-49

# PROMINENT PERSONALITIES

The following select list of prominent persons of Michigan has been selected to indicate the valuable contributions they have made to American life.

BAILEY, James Anthony
  b. Detroit, Mich., July 4, 1847
  d. 1906
  connected with Robinson and Lake Show
  connected with Nashville, Tenn. Theater,
   1863
  Partner, Cooper & Bailey Circus, 1873
  Circus consolidated with P. T. Barnum,
   1881

BROWN, Henry Billings
  b. South Lee, Mass., March 2, 1836
  d. Washington, D. C., September 4,
   1913
  Deputy U. S. Marshal, 1861-63
  Assistant U. S. attorney for Eastern
   District of Michigan, 1863-68
  Judge, Circuit Court, Wayne County,
   Mich., 1868-75
  U. S. District Judge, Easter District
   of Michigan, 1875-90
  Associate Justice, U. S. Supreme Court,
   1890-1906

BURTON, Frederick Russell
  b. Jonesville, Mich., February 23, 1861
  d. 1909
  Author: Shifting Sands, 1898
     Her Wedding Interlude, 1902
  Composer: "Hiawatha," 1898
     "The Legend of Sleepy Hol-
      low," 1900
     "Inauguration Ode" (com-
      posed for second inaugu-
      ration of President William
      McKinley), 1901
     "An Indian Campfire," 1903

CHAPIN, Roy Dikeman
  b. Lansing, Mich., February 23, 1880
  d. February 16, 1936
  Connected with automobile business in
   Detroit, Mich., from 1901
  General sales manager, Olds Motor Works,
   1904-06
  organizer, E. R. Thomas-Detroit Co., 1906
  Treasurer and general manager, E. R.
   Thomas-Detroit Co., 1906-08

Treasurer and general manager of Chalmers-
Detroit Motor Co. (successor of E. R.
Thomas-Detroit Co.), 1908-10
President, Hudson Motor Car Co., 1910-23
Chairman of Board, Hudson Motor Car Co.,
1923-33
Secretary of Commerce, Administration
of President Herbert Hoover, 1932-33

FORD, Henry
b. Dearborn Township, Mich., July 30,
1863
d. April 7, 1947
Chief engineer Edison Illuminating Co.
Organizer, Ford Motor Company, 1903
President, Ford Motor Company
Announced profit-sharing plan for em-
ployees, 1914
Appointed member Wage Umpire Board by
President Woodrow Wilson
Author: My Life and Work, 1925
Today and Tomorrow, 1926
Moving Forward, 1931

INGERSOLL, Robert Hawley
b. Delta, Mich., December 26, 1859
d. September 4, 1928
Manufacturer of rubber stamps, 1880
Ran mail order business
Conceived concept and began manufacture
of "dollar watch," 1892
President and general manager, Robert
H. Ingersoll & Bro.
President, New Era Manufacturing Co.

NOBLE, Alfred
b. Livonia, Mich., August 7, 1844
d. April 19, 1914
Civil engineer - supervised construction
of important railway and other bridges
across Mississippi River and elsewhere,
1886-1904
Member, Isthmian Canal Commission, 1899-1903
Member, Board of consulting engineers,
Panama Canal, 1905

PENFIELD, William Lawrence
b. Dover, Mich., April 2, 1846
d. 1909
Member, Republican State Committee, 1884
Presidential elector and electoral
messenger, 1888

Delegate, Republican National Convention,
    1892
Judge, 35th Circuit of Indiana, 1894-97
Solicitor, U. S. Department of State,
    1897-1905
Counsel for United States in various
    international cases

RYERSON, Martin Antoine
    b. Grand Rapids, Mich., October 26,
        1856
    d. August 11, 1932
    Director Northern Trust Co., Elgin Na-
        tional Watch Co.
    President and honorary president, Board
        of Trustees, University of Chicago
    Vice President, Field Museum of Natural
        History

# FIRST STATE CONSTITUTION

## CONSTITUTION OF MICHIGAN—1835.

*In convention, begun at the city of Detroit, on the second Monday of May, in the year one thousand eight hundred and thirty-five:*

*We, the people of the Territory of Michigan, as established by the act of Congress of the eleventh of January, eighteen hundred and five, in conformity to the fifth article of the ordinance providing for the government of the territory of the United States north-west of the river Ohio, believing that the time has arrived when our present political condition ought to cease, and the right of self-government be asserted; and availing ourselves of that provision of the aforesaid ordinance of the Congress of the United States of the thirteenth day of July, seventeen hundred and eighty-seven, and the acts of Congress passed in accordance therewith, which entitled us to admission into the Union, upon a condition which has been fulfilled, do, by onr delegates in convention assembled, mutually agree to form ourselves into a free and independent State, by the style and title of "The State of Michigan," and do ordain and establish the following constitution for the government of the same:*

### ARTICLE I.

SECTION 1. All political power is inherent in the people.

SEC. 2. Government is instituted for the protection, security, and benefit of the people; and they have the right at all times to alter or reform the same, and to abolish one form of government and establish another, whenever the public good requires it.

SEC. 3. No man or set of men are entitled to exclusive or separate privileges.

SEC. 4. Every person has a right to worship Almighty God according to the dictates of his own conscience; and no person can of right be compelled to attend, erect, or support, against his will, any place of religious worship, or pay any tithes, taxes, or other rates for the support of any minister of the gospel or teacher of religion.

SEC. 5. No money shall be drawn from the treasury for the benefit of religious societies, or theological or religious seminaries.

SEC. 6. The civil and political rights, privileges, and capacities of no individual shall be diminished or enlarged on account of his opinions or belief concerning matters of religion.

SEC. 7. Every person may freely speak, write, and publish his sentiments on all subjects, being responsible for the abuse of that right; and no laws shall be passed to restrain or abridge the liberty of speech or of the press. In all prosecutions or indictments for libels, the truth may be given in evidence to the jury; and if it shall appear to the jury that the matter charged as libellous is true, and was published with good motives and for justifiable ends, the party shall be acquitted; and the jury shall have the right to determine the law and the fact.

SEC. 8. The person, houses, papers, and possessions of every individual shall be secure from unreasonable searches and seizures; and no warrant to search any place, or to seize any person or things, shall issue without describing them, nor without probable cause, supported by oath or affirmation.

SEC. 9. The right of trial by jury shall remain inviolate.

SEC. 10. In all criminal prosecutions, the accused shall have the right to a speedy and public trial by an impartial jury of the vicinage; to be confronted with the witnesses against him; to have compulsory process for obtaining witnesses in his favor; to have the assistance of counsel for his defence; and in all civil cases, in which personal liberty may be involved, the trial by jury shall not be refused.

SEC. 11. No person shall be held to answer for a criminal offence, unless on the presentment or indictment of a grand jury, except in cases of impeachment, or in cases cognizable by justices of the peace, or arising in the army or militia when in actual service in time of war or public danger.

SEC. 12. No person for the same offence shall be twice put in jeopardy of punishment; all persons shall, before conviction, be bailable by sufficient sureties, except for capital offences, when the proof is evident or the presumption great; and the privilege of the writ of *habeas corpus* shall not be suspended, unless when, in case of rebellion or invasion, the public safety may require it.

SEC. 13. Every person has a right to bear arms for the defence of himself and the State.

SEC. 14. The military shall, in all cases and at all times, be in strict subordination to the civil power.

SEC. 15. No soldier shall, in time of peace, be quartered in any house without the consent of the owner, nor in time of war, but in a manner prescribed by law.

SEC. 16. Treason against the State shall consist only in levying war against it, or in adhering to its enemies, giving them aid and comfort; no person shall be convicted of treason, unless on the testimony of two witnesses to the same overt act, or on confession in open court.

SEC. 17. No bill of attainder, *ex post facto* law, or law impairing the obligation of contracts, shall be passed.

SEC. 18. Excessive bail shall not be required; excessive fines shall not be imposed; and cruel and unjust punishments shall not be inflicted.

SEC. 19. The property of no person shall be taken for public use, without just compensation therefor.

SEC. 20. The people shall have the right freely to assemble together to consult for the common good, to instruct their representatives, and to petition the legislature for redress of grievances.

SEC. 21. All acts of the legislature, contrary to this or any other article of this constitution, shall be void.

## ARTICLE II.

### ELECTORS.

SECTION 1. In all elections, every white male citizen above the age of twenty-one years, having resided in the State six months next preceding any election, shall be entitled to vote at such election; and every white male inhabitant of the age aforesaid, who may be a resident of the State at the time of the signing of this constitution, shall have the right of voting as aforesaid; but no such citizen or inhabitant shall be entitled to vote except in the district, county, or township in which he shall actually reside at the time of such election.

SEC. 2. All votes shall be given by ballot, except for such township officers as may, by law, be directed to be otherwise chosen.

SEC. 3. Electors shall, in all cases except treason, felony, or breach of the peace, be privileged from arrest during their attendance at elections, and in going to and returning from the same.

SEC. 4. No elector shall be obliged to do military duty on the days of election, except in time of war or public danger.

SEC. 5. No person shall be deemed to have lost his residence in this State by reason of his absence on business of the United States, or of this State.

SEC. 6. No soldier, seaman, or marine, in the Army or Navy of the United States, shall be deemed a resident of this State in consequence of being stationed in any military or naval place within the same.

## ARTICLE III.

### DIVISION OF THE POWERS OF GOVERNMENT.

The powers of the government shall be divided into three distinct departments: the legislative, the executive, and the judicial; and one department shall never exercise the powers of another, except in such cases as are expressly provided for in this constitution.

## ARTICLE IV.

### LEGISLATIVE DEPARTMENT.

SECTION 1. The legislative power shall be vested in a senate and house of representatives.

SEC. 2. The number of the members of the house of representatives shall never be less than forty-eight, nor more than one hundred; and the senate shall, at all times, equal in number one-third of the house of representatives, as nearly as may be.

SEC. 3. The legislature shall provide by law for an enumeration of the inhabitants of this State in the years eighteen hundred and thirty-seven and eighteen hundred and forty-five, and every ten years after the said last-mentioned time; and at their first session after each enumeration so made as aforesaid, and also after each enumeration made by the authority of the United States, the legislature shall apportion anew the representatives and senators among the several counties and districts, according to the number of white inhabitants.

SEC. 4. The representatives shall be chosen annually on the first Monday of November, and on the following day, by the electors of the several counties or districts into which the State shall be divided for that purpose. Each organized county shall be entitled to at least one representative; but no county hereafter organized shall be entitled to a separate representative, until it shall have attained a population equal to the ratio of representation hereafter established.

SEC. 5. The senators shall be chosen for two years, at the same time and in the same manner as the representatives are required to be chosen. At the first session of the legislature under this constitution, they shall be divided by lot from their respective districts, as nearly as may be, into two equal classes; the seats of the senators of the first class shall be vacated at the expiration of the first year, and of the second class at the expiration of the second year; so that one-half thereof, as nearly as may be, shall be chosen annually thereafter.

SEC. 6. The State shall be divided, at each new apportionment, into a number of not less than four, nor more than eight, senatorial districts, to be always composed of contiguous territory, so that each district shall elect an equal number of senators annually, as nearly as may be; and no county shall be divided in the formation of such districts.

SEC. 7. Senators and representatives shall be citizens of the United States, and be qualified electors in the respective counties and districts which they represent; and a removal from their respective counties or districts shall be deemed a vacation of their seats.

SEC. 8. No person holding any office under the United States, or of this State, officers of the militia, justices of the peace, associate judges of the circuit and county courts, and postmasters excepted, shall be eligible to either house of the legislature.

SEC. 9. Senators and representatives shall, in all cases except treason, felony, or breach of the peace, be privileged from arrest, nor shall they be subject to any civil process, during the session of the legislature, nor for fifteen days next before the commencement and after the termination of each session.

SEC. 10. A majority of each house shall constitute a quorum to do business; but a smaller number may adjourn from day to day, and may compel the attendance of absent members, in such manner and under such penalties as each house may provide. Each house shall choose its own officers.

SEC. 11. Each house shall determine the rules of its proceedings, and judge of the qualifications, elections, and returns of its own members; and may, with the concurrence of two-thirds of all the members elected, expel a member; but no member shall be expelled a second time for the same cause, nor for any cause known to his constituents antecedent to his election.

SEC. 12. Each house shall keep a journal of its proceedings, and publish the same, except such parts as may require secrecy; and the yeas and nays of the members of either house, on any question, shall, at the request of one-fifth of the members present, be entered on the journal. Any member of either house shall have liberty to dissent from and protest against any act or resolution which he may think injurious to the public or an individual, and have the reasons of his dissent entered on the journal.

SEC. 13. In all elections by either or both houses, the votes shall be given *viva voce;* and all votes on nominations made to the senate shall be taken by yeas and nays, and published with the journals of its proceedings.

SEC. 14. The doors of each house shall be open, except when the public welfare shall require secrecy; neither house shall, without the consent of the other, adjourn for more than three days, nor to any other place than that where the legislature may then be in session.

SEC. 15. Any bill may originate in either house of the legislature.

SEC. 16. Every bill passed by the legislature shall, before it becomes a law, be presented to the governor; if he approve, he shall sign it; but if not, he shall return it with his objections to that house in which it originated, who shall enter the objections at large upon their journal, and proceed to reconsider it. If, after such reconsideration, two-thirds of all the members present agree to pass the bill, it shall be sent, with the objections, to the other house, by whom it shall likewise be reconsidered; and if approved also by two-thirds of all the members present in that house, it shall become a law; but in such cases, the votes of both houses shall be determined by yeas and nays, and the names of the members voting for or against the bill shall be entered on the journals of each house respectively. And if any bill be not returned by the governor within ten days, Sundays excepted, after it has been presented to him, the same shall become a law, in like manner as if he had signed it, unless the legislature, by their adjournment, prevent its return, in which case it shall not become a law.

SEC. 17. Every resolution to which the concurrence of the senate and house of representatives may be necessary, except in cases of adjournment, shall be presented to the governor, and, before the same shall take effect, shall be proceeded upon in the same manner as in the case of a bill.

SEC. 18. The members of the legislature shall receive for their services a compensation to be ascertained by law, and paid out of the public treasury; but no increase of the compensation shall take effect during the term for which the members of either house shall have been elected; and such compensation shall never exceed three dollars a day.

SEC. 19. No member of the legislature shall receive any civil appointment from the governor and senate, or from the legislature, during the term for which he is elected.

SEC. 20. The governor shall issue writs of election to fill such vacancies as may occur in the senate and house of representatives.

SEC. 21. The legislature shall meet on the first Monday in January in every year, and at no other period, unless otherwise directed by law, or provided for in this constitution.

SEC. 22. The style of the laws of this State shall be, *"Be it enacted by the senate and house of representatives of the State of Michigan."*

## ARTICLE V.
### EXECUTIVE DEPARTMENT.

SECTION 1. The supreme executive power shall be vested in a governor, who shall hold his office for two years; and a lieutenant-governor shall be chosen at the same time and for the same term.

SEC. 2. No person shall be eligible to the office of governor or lieutenant-governor, who shall not have been five years a citizen of the United States, and a resident of this State two years next preceding the election.

SEC. 3. The governor and lieutenant-governor shall be elected by the electors at the times and places of choosing members of the legislature. The persons having the highest number of votes for governor and lieutenant-governor shall be elected; but in case two or more have an equal and the highest number of votes for governor or lieutenant-governor, the legislature shall, by joint vote, choose one of the said persons, so having an equal and the highest number of votes, for governor or lieutenant-governor.

SEC. 4. The returns of every election for governor and lieutenant-governor shall be sealed up and transmitted to the seat of government, by the returning-officers, directed to the president of the senate, who shall open and publish them in the presence of the members of both houses.

SEC. 5. The governor shall be commander-in-chief of the militia, and of the army and navy of this State.

SEC. 6. He shall transact all executive business with the officers of government, civil and military; and may require information, in writing, from the officers in the executive department, upon any subject relating to the duties of their respective offices.

SEC. 7. He shall take care that the laws be faithfully executed.

SEC. 8. He shall have power to convene the legislature on extraordinary occasions. He shall communicate, by message, to the legislature, at every session, the condition of the State, and recommend such matters to them as he shall deem expedient.

SEC. 9. He shall have power to adjourn the legislature to such time as he may think proper, in case of a disagreement between the two houses with respect to the time of adjournment, but not to a period beyond the next annual meeting.

SEC. 10. He may direct the legislature to meet at some other place than the seat of government, if that shall become, after its adjournment, dangerous from a common enemy or a contagious disease.

SEC. 11. He shall have power to grant reprieves and pardons after conviction, except in cases of impeachment.

SEC. 12. When any office, the appointment to which is vested in the governor and senate, or in the legislature, becomes vacant during the recess of the legislature, the governor shall have power to fill such vacancy by granting a commission, which shall expire at the end of the succeeding session of the legislature.

SEC. 13. In case of the impeachment of the governor, his removal from office, death, resignation, or absence from the State, the powers and duties of the office shall devolve upon the lieutenant-governor until such disability shall cease, or the vacancy be filled.

SEC. 14. If, during the vacancy of the office of governor, the lieutenant-governor shall be impeached, displaced, resign, die, or be absent from the State, the president of the senate *pro tempore* shall act as governor until the vacancy be filled.

SEC. 15. The lieutenant-governor shall, by virtue of his office, be president of the senate; in committee of the whole, he may debate on all questions; and, when there is an equal division, he shall give the casting vote.

SEC. 16. No member of Congress, nor any other person holding office under the United States, or this State, shall execute the office of governor.

SEC. 17. Whenever the office of governor or lieutenant-governor becomes vacant, the person exercising the powers of governor for the time being shall give notice thereof, and the electors shall, at the next succeeding annual election for members of the legislature, choose a person to fill such vacancy.

SEC. 18. The governor shall, at stated times, receive for his services a compensation, which shall neither be increased nor diminished during the term for which he has been elected.

SEC. 19. The lieutenant-governor, except when acting as governor, and the president of the senate *pro tempore*, shall each receive the same compensation as shall be allowed to the speaker of the house of representatives.

SEC. 20. A great seal for the State shall be provided by the governor, which shall contain the device and inscriptions represented and described in the papers relating thereto, signed by the president of the convention, and deposited in the office of the secretary of the territory. It shall be kept by the secretary of state; and all official acts of the governor, his approbation of the laws excepted, shall be thereby authenticated.

SEC. 21. All grants and commissions shall be in the name and by the authority of the people of the State of Michigan.

# ARTICLE VI.

### JUDICIAL DEPARTMENT.

SECTION 1. The judicial power shall be vested in one supreme court, and in such other courts as the legislature may from time to time establish.

SEC. 2. The judges of the supreme court shall hold their offices for the term of seven years; they shall be nominated and, by and with the advice and consent of the senate, appointed by the governor. They shall receive an adequate compensation, which shall not be diminished during their continuance in office. But they shall receive no fees nor perquisites of office, nor hold any other office of profit or trust under the authority of this State, or of the United States.

SEC. 3. A court of probate shall be established in each of the organized counties.

SEC. 4. Judges of all county courts, associate judges of circuit courts, and judges of probate shall be elected by the qualified electors of the county in which they reside, and shall hold their offices for four years.

SEC. 5. The supreme court shall appoint their clerk or clerks; and the electors of each county shall elect a clerk, to be denominated a county clerk, who shall hold his office for the term of two years, and shall perform the duties of clerk to all the courts of record to be held in each county, except the supreme court and court of probate.

SEC. 6. Each township may elect four justices of the peace, who shall hold their offices for four years; and whose powers and duties shall be defined and regulated by law. At their first election they shall be classed and divided by lot into numbers one, two, three, and four, to be determined in such manner as shall be prescribed by law, so that one justice shall be annually elected in each township thereafter. A removal of any justice from the township in which he was elected shall vacate his office. In all incorporated towns, or cities, it shall be competent for the legislature to increase the number of justices.

SEC. 7. The style of all process shall be, "In the name of the people of the State of Michigan;" and all indictments shall conclude, "Against the peace and dignity of the same."

# ARTICLE VII.

### CERTAIN STATE AND COUNTY OFFICERS.

SECTION 1. There shall be a secretary of state, who shall hold his office for two years, and who shall be appointed by the governor, by and with the advice and consent of the senate. He shall keep a fair record of the official acts of the legislative and executive departments of the government; and shall, when required, lay the same, and all matters relative thereto, before either branch of the legislature; and shall perform such other duties as shall be assigned him by law.

SEC. 2. A State treasurer shall be appointed by a joint vote of the two houses of the legislature, and shall hold his office for the term of two years.

SEC. 3. There shall be an auditor-general and an attorney-general for the State, and a prosecuting attorney for each of the respective counties, who shall hold their offices for two years, and who shall be appointed by the governor, by and with the advice and consent of the senate, and whose powers and duties shall be prescribed by law.

SEC. 4. There shall be a sheriff, a county treasurer, and one or more coroners, a register of deeds, and a county surveyor, chosen by the electors in each of the several counties, once in every two years, and as often as vacancies shall happen. The sheriff shall hold no other office, and shall not be capable of holding the office of sheriff longer than four in any term of six years. He may be required by law to renew his security from time to time, and in default of giving such security, his office shall be deemed vacant; but the county shall never be made responsible for the acts of the sheriff.

## ARTICLE VIII.

### IMPEACHMENTS AND REMOVALS FROM OFFICE.

SECTION 1. The house of representatives shall have the sole power of impeaching all civil officers of the State for corrupt conduct in office, or for crimes and misdemeanors; but a majority of all the members elected shall be necessary to direct an impeachment.

SEC. 2. All impeachments shall be tried by the senate. When the governor or lieutenant-governor shall be tried, the chief justice of the supreme court shall preside. Before the trial of an impeachment, the members of the court shall take an oath or affirmation truly and impartially to try and determine the charge in question according to the evidence; and no person shall be convicted without the concurrence of two-thirds of the members present. Judgment, in cases of impeachment, shall not extend further than to removal from office; but the party convicted shall be liable to indictment and punishment according to law.

SEC. 3. For any reasonable cause, which shall not be sufficient ground for the impeachment of the judges of any of the courts, the governor shall remove any of them on the address of two-thirds of each branch of the legislature; but the cause or causes for which such removal may be required shall be stated at length in the address.

SEC. 4. The legislature shall provide by law for the removal of justices of the peace, and other county and township officers, in such manner and for such cause as to them shall seem just and proper.

## ARTICLE IX.

### MILITIA.

SECTION 1. The legislature shall provide by law for organizing and disciplining the militia, in such manner as they shall deem expedient, not incompatible with the Constitution and laws of the United States.

SEC. 2. The legislature shall provide for the efficient discipline of the officers, commissioned and non-commissioned, and musicians, and may provide by law for the organization and discipline of volunteer companies.

SEC. 3. Officers of the militia shall be elected or appointed in such manner as the legislature shall from time to time direct, and shall be commissioned by the governor.

SEC. 4. The governor shall have power to call forth the militia, to execute the laws of the State, to suppress insurrections, and repel invasions.

## ARTICLE X.

### EDUCATION.

SECTION 1. The governor shall nominate and, by and with the advice and consent of the legislature in joint vote, shall appoint a superintendent of public instruction, who shall hold his office for two years, and whose duties shall be prescribed by law.

SEC. 2. The legislature shall encourage, by all suitable means, the promotion of intellectual, scientific, and agricultural improvement. The proceeds of all lands that have been or hereafter may be granted by the United States to this State, for the support of schools, which shall hereafter be sold or disposed of, shall be and remain a perpetual fund, the interest of which, together with the rents of all such unsold lands, shall be inviolably appropriated to the support of schools throughout the State.

SEC. 3. The legislature shall provide for a system of common schools, by which a school shall be kept up and supported in each school-district at least three months in every year; and any school-district neglecting to keep up and support such a school may be deprived of its equal proportion of the interest of the public fund.

SEC. 4. As soon as the circumstances of the State will permit, the legislature shall provide for the establishment of libraries; one at least in each township; and the money which shall be paid by persons as an equivalent for exemption from military duty, and the clear proceeds of all fines assessed in the several counties for any breach of the penal laws, shall be exclusively applied to the support of said libraries.

Sec. 5. The legislature shall take measures for the protection, improvement, or other disposition of such lands as have been or may hereafter be reserved or granted by the United States to this State for the support of a university, and the funds accruing from the rents or sale of such lands, or from any other source, for the purpose aforesaid, shall be and remain a permanent fund for the support of said university, with such branches as the public convenience may hereafter demand for the promotion of literature, the arts and sciences, and as may be authorized by the terms of such grant. And it shall be the duty of the legislature, as soon as may be, to provide effectual means for the improvement and permanent security of the funds of said university.

## ARTICLE XI.

### PROHIBITION OF SLAVERY.

Neither slavery nor involuntary servitude shall ever be introduced into this State, except for the punishment of crimes of which the party shall have been duly convicted.

## ARTICLE XII.

### MISCELLANEOUS PROVISIONS.

Section 1. Members of the legislature, and all officers, executive and judicial, except such inferior officers as may by law be exempted, shall, before they enter on the duties of their respective offices, take and subscribe the following oath or affirmation: "I do solemnly swear [or affirm, as the case may be] that I will support the Constitution of the United States and the constitution of this State, and that I will faithfully discharge the duties of the office of ———, according to the best of my ability." And no other oath, declaration, or test shall be required as a qualification for any office or public trust.

Sec. 2. The legislature shall pass no act of incorporation, unless with the assent of at least two-thirds of each house.

Sec. 3. Internal improvement shall be encouraged by the government of this State; and it shall be the duty of the legislature, as soon as may be, to make provision by law for ascertaining the proper objects of improvement in relation to roads, canals, and navigable waters; and it shall also be their duty to provide by law for an equal, systematic, and economical application of the funds which may be appropriated to these objects.

Sec. 4. No money shall be drawn from the treasury but in consequence of appropriations made by law; and an accurate statement of the receipts and expenditures of the public money shall be attached to and published with the laws annually.

Sec. 5. Divorces shall not be granted by the legislature, but the legislature may by law authorize the higher courts to grant them, under such restrictions as they may deem expedient.

Sec. 6. No lottery shall be authorized by this State, nor shall the sale of lottery-tickets be allowed.

Sec. 7. No county now organized by law shall ever be reduced, by the organization of new counties, to less than four hundred square miles.

See. 8. The governor, secretary of state, treasurer, and auditor-general shall keep their offices at the seat of government.

Sec. 9. The seat of government for this State shall be at Detroit, or at such other place or places as may be prescribed by law, until the year eighteen hundred and forty-seven, when it shall be permanently located by the legislature.

Sec. 10. The first governor and lieutenant-governor shall hold their offices until the first Monday of January, eighteen hundred and thirty-eight, and until others shall be elected and qualified, and thereafter they shall hold their offices for two years, and until their successors shall be elected and qualified.

Sec. 11. When a vacancy shall happen, occasioned by the death, resignation, or removal from office of any person holding office under this State, the successor thereto shall hold his office for the period which his predecessor had to serve, and no longer, unless again chosen or reappointed.

## ARTICLE XIII.

### MODE OF AMENDING AND REVISING THE CONSTITUTION.

SECTION 1. Any amendment or amendments to this constitution may be proposed in the senate or house of representatives; and if the same shall be agreed to by a majority of the members elected to each of the two houses, such proposed amendment or amendments shall be entered on their journals, with the yeas and nays taken thereon, and referred to the legislature then next to be chosen, and shall be published for three months previous to the time of making such choice. And if in the legislature next chosen as aforesaid such proposed amendment or amendments shall be agreed to by two-thirds of all the members elected to each house, then it shall be the duty of the legislature to submit such proposed amendment or amendments to the people, in such manner and at such time as the legislature shall prescribe; and if the people shall approve and ratify such amendment or amendments, by a majority of the electors qualified to vote for members of the legislature voting thereon, such amendment or amendments shall become part of the constitution.

SEC. 2. And if at any time two-thirds of the senate and house of representatives shall think it necessary to revise or change this entire constitution, they shall recommend to the electors at the next election for members of the legislature to vote for or against a convention; and if it shall appear that a majority of the electors voting at such election have voted in favor of calling a convention, the legislature shall at its next session provide by law for calling a convention to be holden within six months after the passage of such law; and such convention shall consist of a number of members not less than that of both branches of the legislature.

## SCHEDULE.

SECTION. 1. That no inconvenience may arise from a change of the territorial government to a permanent State government, it is declared that all writs, actions, prosecutions, contracts, claims, and rights of individuals and of bodies-corporate shall continue as if no change had taken place in this government; and all process which may, before the organization of the judicial department under this constitution, be issued under the authority of the Territory of Michigan, shall be as valid as if issued in the name of the State.

SEC. 2. All laws now in force in the Territory of Michigan, which are not repugnant to this constitution, shall remain in force until they expire by their own limitations, or be altered or repealed by the legislature.

SEC. 3. All fines, penalties, forfeitures, and escheats accruing to the Territory of Michigan shall accrue to the use of the State.

SEC. 4. All recognizances heretofore taken, or which may be taken before the organization of the judicial department under this constitution, shall remain valid, and shall pass over to and may be prosecuted in the name of the State. And all bonds executed to the governor of this Territory, or to any other officer in his official capacity, shall pass over to the governor or other proper State authority, and to their successors in office, for the uses therein respectively expressed, and may be sued for and recovered accordingly. All criminal prosecutions and penal actions which have arisen or which may arise before the organization of the judicial department under this constitution, and which shall then be depending, may be prosecuted to judgment and execution in the name of the State.

SEC. 5. All officers, civil and military, now holding their offices and appointments in this Territory under the authority of the United States, or under the authority of this Territory, shall continue to hold and exercise their respective offices and appointments until superseded under this constitution.

SEC. 6. The first election for governor, lieutenant-governor, members of the State legislature, and a Representative in the Congress of the United States, shall be held on the first Monday in October next, and on the succeeding day. And the president of the convention shall issue writs to the sheriffs of the several counties or districts, or, in case of vacancy, to the coroners, requiring them to cause such election to be held on the days aforesaid, in their respective counties or districts. The election shall be conducted in the manner prescribed, and by the township officers designated as inspectors of elections, and the returns made as required by the existing laws of the Territory, or by this constitution: *Provided, however*, That the returns of the several townships in the district composed of the unorganized counties of Ottawa, Ionia, Kent, and Clinton shall be made to the clerk of the township of Kent in said district, and the said township clerk shall perform the same duties as by the existing laws of the Territory devolve upon the clerks of the several counties in similar cases.

SEC. 7. The first meeting of the legislature shall be at the city of Detroit, on the first Monday in November next, with power to adjourn to any other place.

SEC. 8. All county and township officers shall continue to hold their respective offices, unless removed by the competent authority, until the legislature shall, in conformity to the provisions of this constitution, provide for the holding of elections to fill such offices respectively.

SEC. 9. This constitution shall be submitted, at the election to be held on the first Monday in October next, and on the succeeding day, for ratification or rejection, to the electors qualified by this constitution to vote at all elections; and if the same be ratified by the said electors, the same shall become the constitution of the State of Michigan. At the election aforesaid, on such of the ballots as are for the said constitution, shall be written or printed the word "Yes," and on those which are against the ratification of said constitution, the word "No." And the returns of the votes on the question of ratification or rejection of said constitution shall be made to the president of this convention at any time before the first Monday in November next, and a digest of the same communicated by him to the senate and house of representatives on that day.

SEC. 10. And if this constitution shall be ratified by the people of Michigan, the president of this convention shall, immediately after the same shall be ascertained, cause a fair copy thereof, together with an authenticated copy of the act of the legislative council, entitled "An act to enable the people of Michigan to form a constitution and State government, approved January 26, 1835, providing for the calling of this convention, and also a copy of so much of the last census of this Territory as exhibits the number of the free inhabitants of that part thereof which is comprised within the limits in said constitution defined as the boundaries of the proposed State of Michigan, to be forwarded to the President of the United States, together with an expression of the decided opinion of this convention that the number of the free inhabitants of said proposed State now exceeds the number requisite to constitute two congressional districts, and the respectful request of this convention, in behalf of the people of Michigan, that all said matters may be by him laid before the Congress of the United States at their next session.

SEC. 11. In case of the failure of the president of this convention to perform the duties prescribed by this constitution, by reason of his absence, death, or from any other cause, said duties shall be performed by the secretaries of this convention.

SEC. 12. Until the first enumeration shall be made, as directed by this constitution, the county of Wayne shall be entitled to eight representatives; the county of Monroe to four representatives; the county of Washtenaw to seven representatives; the county of Saint Clair to one representative; the county of Saint Joseph to two representatives; the county of Berrien to one representative; the county of Calhoun to one representative; the county of Jackson to one representative; the county of Cass to two representatives; the county of Oakland to six representatives; the county of Macomb to three representatives; the county of Lenawee to four representatives; the county of Kalamazoo, and the unorganized counties of Allegan and Barry, to two representatives; the county of Branch to one representative; the county of Hillsdale to one representative; the county of Lapeer to one representative; the county of Saginaw, and the unorganized counties of Genesee and Shiawasse, to one representative; the county of Michilimackinac to one representative; the county of Chippewa to one representative; and the unorganized counties of Ottawa, Kent, Ionia, and Clinton to one representative.

And for the election of senators the State shall be divided into five districts, and the apportionment shall be as follows: The county of Wayne shall compose the first district, and elect three senators; the counties of Monroe and Lenawee shall compose the second district, and elect three senators; the counties of Hillsdale, Branch, Saint Joseph, Cass, Berrien, Kalamazoo, and Calhoun shall compose the third district, and elect three senators; the counties of Washtenaw and Jackson shall compose the fourth district, and elect three senators; and the counties of Oakland, Lapeer, Saginaw, Macomb, Saint Clair, Michilimackinac, and Chippewa shall compose the fifth district, and elect four senators.

Any country attached to any county for judicial purposes, if not otherwise represented, shall be considered as forming part of such county, so far as regards elections for the purpose of representation in the legislature.

JOHN BIDDLE, *President.*

# SELECTED DOCUMENTS


The documents selected for this section have been chosen to reflect the interests or attitudes of the contemporary observer or writer. Documents relating specifically to the constitutional development of Michigan will be found in volume five of <u>Sources and Documents of United States Constitutions</u>, a companion reference collection to the Columbia University volumes previously cited.

## THE SURRENDER OF DETROIT

Genetal Hull justifies his
surrender of Detroit.  Lewis
Cass describes in a dispara-
ging manner General Hull's
action.

Source:  <u>America: Great Crises in Our History Told by
Its Makers</u>.  Chicago: Issued by Americanization Department, Veterans of Foreign Wars of the United States,
1925.

## THE SURRENDER OF DETROIT

### GENERAL HULL'S STATEMENT IN HIS OWN DEFENSE

*FOLLOWING the declaration of war in 1812, General Hull marched his troops into Canada.  There he remained inactive while the British gathered their forces and when they made an attack he surrendered.*

*Hull had evidently been much shaken by the recent massacre of detachments of his troops, and historians are inclined to lighten the blame given to him at the time, but there is no doubt that in surrendering his command he left a vast territory defenseless.*

*This letter from General Hull to the Secretary of War was dated at Fort George, August 16th, 1812,—ten days after the surrender for which he was court-martialed and sentenced to death. This, however, was commuted because of his age.*

*The disfavor in which Hull was held by his fellow officers is shown by this report to the War Department made a few weeks later by Lewis Cass who became Governor of the territory in 1813 and later Secretary of War and Minister to France.*

ENCLOSED are the articles of capitulation, by which the Fort of Detroit has been surrendered to major general Brock, commanding his Britannic majesty's forces in Upper Canada, and by which the troops have become prisoners of war. My situation at present forbids me from detailing the particular causes which have led to this unfortunate event.  I will, however, generally observe, that after the surrender of Michilimakinac, almost every tribe and nation of Indians, excepting a part of the Miamies and Delawares, north from beyond Lake Superior, west from beyond the Mississippi, south from the Ohio and Wabash, and east from every part of Upper Canada, and from all the intermediate country, joined in open hostility, under the British standard, against the army I commanded, contrary to the most solemn assurances of a large portion of them to remain neutral: even the Ottawa chiefs from Arbecrotch, who formed the delegation to Washington the last summer, in whose friendship I know you had great confidence, are among the hostile tribes, and several of them distinguished leaders. Among the vast number of chiefs who led the hostile bands, Tecumseh, Marpot, Logan, Walk-in-the-Water, Split Log, &c., are considered the principals. This numerous assemblage of savages, under the entire influence and direction of the British commander, enabled him totally to obstruct the only communication which I had with my country. This communication had been opened from the settlements in the state of Ohio, two hundred miles through a wilderness, by the fatigues of the army, which I marched to the frontier on the river Detroit. The body of the lake being commanded by the British armed ships, and the shores and rivers by gun boats, the army was totally deprived of all communication by water. On this extensive road it depended for transportation of provisions, military stores, medicine, clothing, and every other supply, on pack horses—all its operations were successful until its arrival at Detroit, and in a few days it passed into the enemy's country, and all opposition seemed to drop before it. One month it remained in possession of this country, and was fed from its resources. In different directions, detachments penetrated sixty miles in the settled part of the province, and the inhabitants seemed satisfied with the change of situation, which appeared to be taking place; the militia from Amherstburg were daily deserting, and the whole country, then under the control of the army, was asking for protection. The Indians, generally, in the first instance, appeared to be neutralized, and determined to take no part in the contest. The fort of Amherstburg was eighteen miles below my encampment. Not a single cannon or mortar was on wheels suitable to carry before this place. I consulted my officers, whether it was expedient to make an attempt on it with the bayonet alone, without cannon,

to make a break in the first instance. The council I
called was of the opinion it was not. The greatest
industry was exerted in making preparation, and it
was not until the 7th of August, that two 24 pounders, and three howitzers were prepared. It was then
my intention to have proceeded on the enterprise.
While the operations of the army were delayed by
these preparations, the clouds of adversity had been
for some time and seemed still thickly to be gathering
around me. The surrender of Michilimackinac
opened the northern hive of Indians, and they were
swarming down in every direction. Reinforcements
from Niagara had arrived at Amherstburg under the
command of Colonel Proctor. The desertion of the
militia ceased. Besides the reinforcements that came
by water, I received information of a very considerable force under the command of Major Chambers, on
the river Le French, with four field pieces, and collect-
ing the militia on his route, evidently destined for
Amherstburg; and in addition to this combination,
and increase of force, contrary to all my expectations,
the Wyandots, Chippewas, Ottawas, Pottawatamies,
Munsees, Delawares, &c., with whom I had the most
friendly intercourse, at once passed over to Amherstburg, and accepted the tomahawk and scalping knife.
There being now a vast number of Indians at the
British post, they were sent to the river Huron,
Brownstown, and Maguago to intercept my communication. To open this communication, I detached
Major Van Horn of the Ohio volunteers, with two
hundred men, to proceed as far as the river Raisin, under an expectation he would meet Captain Brush with
one hundred and fifty men, volunteers from the state
of Ohio, and a quantity of provision for the army. An
ambuscade was formed at Brownstown, and Major
Van Horn's detachment defeated and returned to
camp without effecting the object of the expedition.
In my letter of the 7th instant you have the particulars of that transaction, with a return of the killed
and wounded. Under this sudden and unexpected
change of things, and having received an express from
General Hall, commanding opposite the British shore
on the Niagara river, by which it appeared that there
was no prospect of a coöperation from that quarter,

and the two senior officers of the artillery having stated to me an opinion that it would be extremely difficult, if not impossible, to pass the Turkey river and river Aux Cannard, with the 24 pounders, and that they could not be transported by water, as the Queen Charlotte, which carried eighteen 24 pounders, lay in the river Detroit above the mouth of the river Aux Cannard; and as it appeared indispensably necessary to open the communication to the river Raisin and the Miami, I found myself compelled to suspend the operation against Amherstburg, and concentrate the main force of the army at Detroit. Fully intending at that time, after the communication was opened, to re-cross the river, and pursue the object at Amherstburg, and strongly desirous of continuing protection to a very large number of the inhabitants of Upper Canada, who had voluntarily accepted it under my proclamation, I established a fortress on the banks of the river, a little below Detroit, calculated for a garrison of 300 men. On the evening of the 7th, and morning of the 8th instant, the army, excepting the garrison of 250 infantry, and a corps of artillerists, all under the command of Major Denny of the Ohio volunteers, re-crossed the river, and encamped at Detroit. In pursuance of the object of opening the communication, on which I considered the existence of the army depending, a detachment of 600 men, under the command of Lieutenant Colonel Miller, was immediately ordered. For a particular account of the proceedings of this detachment, and the memorable battle which was fought at Maguago, which reflects the highest honor on the American arms, I refer you to my letter of the 13th of August instant, a duplicate of which is enclosed, marked G. Nothing however but honor was acquired by this victory; and it is a painful consideration, that the blood of seventy-five gallant men could only open the communication, as far as the points of their bayonets extended. The necessary care of the sick and wounded, and a very severe storm of rain, rendered their return to camp indispensably necessary for their own comfort. Captain Brush, with his small detachment, and the provisions being still at the river Raisin, and in a situation to be destroyed by the savages, on the 13th instant in the evening, I permitted Colonels McArthur and Cass to select from their regiment four hundred of their most effective men, and proceed an upper route through the woods, which I had sent an express to Captain Brush to take, and had directed the militia of the river Raisin to accompany him as a reinforcement. The force of the enemy continually increasing, and the necessity of opening the communication, and acting on the defensive, becoming more apparent, I had, previous to detaching Colonels McArthur and Cass on the 11th instant, evacuated and destroyed the fort on the opposite bank. On the 13th, in the evening, General Brock arrived at Amherstburg about the hour that Colonels McArthur and Cass marched, of which at that time I had received no information. On the 15th I received a summons from him to surrender Fort Detroit, of which the paper marked A is a copy. My answer is marked B. At this time I had received no information from Colonels McArthur and Cass. An express was immediately sent, strongly escorted, with orders for them to return. On the 15th, as soon as General Brock received my letter, his batteries opened on the town and fort, and continued until evening. In the evening all the British ships of war came nearly as far up the river as Sandwich, three miles below Detroit. At daylight on the 16th (at which time I had received no information from Colonels McArthur and Cass, my expresses, sent the evening before, and in the night having been prevented from passing by numerous bodies of Indians) the cannonade re-commenced, and in a short time I received information, that the British army and Indians, were landing below the Spring Wells, under the cover of their ships of war. At this time the whole effective force at my disposal at Detroit did not exceed eight hundred men. Being new troops, and unaccustomed to a camp life; having performed a laborious march; having been engaged in a number of battles and skirmishes, in which many had fallen, and more had received wounds, in addition to which a large number being sick, and unprovided with medicine, and the comforts necessary for their situation; are the general causes by which the strength of the army was thus reduced. The fort at this time was filled with women,

children, and the old and decrepit people of the town
and country; they were unsafe in the town, as it was
entirely open and exposed to the enemy's batteries.
Back of the fort, above or below it, there was no
safety for them on account of the Indians. In the first
instance the enemy's fire was principally directed
against our batteries; towards the close, it was directed against the fort alone, and almost every shot
and shell had their effect.

It now became necessary either to fight the enemy
in the field; collect the whole force in the fort; or
propose terms of capitulation. I could not have carried into the field more than six hundred men, and left
any adequate force in the fort. There were landed at
that time of the enemy a regular force of much more
than that number, and twice the number of Indians.
Considering this great inequality of force I did not
think it expedient to adopt the first measure. The
second must have been attended with a great sacrifice
of blood, and no possible advantage, because the contest could not have been sustained more than a day
for the want of powder, and but a very few days for
the want of provisions. In addition to this, Colonels
McArthur and Cass would have been in a most haz-
ardous situation. I feared nothing but the last alter-
native. I have dared to adopt it. I well know the
high responsibility of the measure, and take the whole
of it on myself. It was dictated by a sense of duty,
and a full conviction of its expediency. The bands of
savages which had then joined the British force were
numerous beyond any former example. Their numbers have since increased, and the history of the bar-
barians of the north of Europe does not furnish ex-
amples of more greedy violence than these savages
have exhibited. A large portion of the brave and gallant officers and men I commanded would cheerfully
have contested until the last cartridge had been ex-
pended, and the bayonets worn to the sockets. I
could not consent to the useless sacrifice of such brave
men, when I knew it was impossible for me to sustain
my situation. It was impossible in the nature of
things that an army could have been furnished with
the necessary supplies of provision, military stores,
clothing and comforts for the sick, or pack horses,

through a wilderness of two hundred miles, filled with hostile savages. It was impossible, sir, that this little army, worn down by fatigue, by sickness, by wounds, and deaths, could have supported itself not only against the collected force of all the northern nations of Indians; but against the united strength of Upper Canada, whose population consists of more than twenty times the number contained in the territory of Michigan, aided by the principal part of the regular forces of the province, and the wealth and influence of the north-west and other trading establishments among the Indians, which have in their employment, and under their entire control, more than two thousand white men. Before I close this despatch, it is a duty I owe to my respectable associates in command, Colonels McArthur, Findlay, Cass, and Lieutenant Colonel Miller, to express my obligations to them for the prompt and judicious manner they have performed their respective duties. If aught has taken place during the campaign, which is honorable to the army, these officers are entitled to a large share of it. If the last act should be disapproved, no part of the censure belongs to them. I have likewise to express my obligation to General Taylor, who has performed the duty of quarter master general, for his great exertions in procuring everything in his department which it was possible to furnish for the convenience of the army; likewise to Brigade Major Jessup for the correct and punctual manner in which he has discharged his duty; and to the army generally for their exertions, and the zeal they have manifested for the public interest. The death of Dr. Foster soon after he arrived at Detroit, was a severe misfortune to the army; it was increased by the capture of the Chachago packet, by which the medicine and hospital stores were lost. He was commencing the best arrangements in the department of which he was the principal, with the very small means he possessed. I was likewise deprived of the necessary services of Captain Partridge by sickness, the only officer of the corps of engineers attached to the army. All the officers and men have gone to their respective homes, excepting the 4th United States' regiment, and a small part of the 1st, and Captain Dyson's company of artillery. Captain Dyson's company was left at Amherstburg, and the others are with me prisoners—they amount to about three hundred and forty. I have only to solicit an investigation of my conduct, as early as my situation and the state of things will admit; and to add the further request, that the government will not be unmindful of my associates in captivity, and of the families of those brave men who have fallen in the contest.

I have the honor to be, very respectfully,

Your most obedient servant,

Wm. Hull.

### Cass Describes Hull's Ignominy

HAVING been ordered on to this place by Colonel McArthur, for the purpose of communicating to the government such particulars respecting the expedition lately commanded by Brigadier General Hull and its disastrous result, as might enable them correctly to appreciate the conduct of the officers and men, and to develop the causes which produced so foul a stain upon the national character, I have the honor to submit to your consideration the following statement:

When the forces landed in Canada, they landed with an ardent zeal, and stimulated with the hope of conquest. No enemy appeared within view of us, and had an immediate and vigorous attack been made upon Malden, it would doubtless have fallen an easy victory. I knew General Hull afterwards declared he regretted this attack had not been made, and he had every reason to believe success would have crowned his efforts. The reasons given for delaying our operations was to mount our heavy cannon, and to afford to the Canadian militia time and opportunity to quit an obnoxious service. In the course of two weeks the number of their militia who were embodied, had decreased by desertion, from six hundred to one hundred men; and, in the course of three weeks, the cannon were mounted, the ammunition fixed, and every preparation made for an immediate investment of the fort. At a council, at which were present all the field officers, and which was held two days before our preparations were completed, it was unanimously agreed to make an immediate attempt to accomplish the object of the expedition. If by waiting two days we could have the service of our heavy artillery, it was agreed to wait; if not, it was determined to go without it and attempt the place by storm. This opinion appeared to correspond with the views of the general, and the day was appointed for commencing our march. He declared to me that he considered himself pledged to lead the army to Malden. The ammunition was placed in the wagons; the cannon were embarked on board the floating batteries, and every requisite article was prepared. The spirit and zeal, the ardor and animation displayed by the officers and men on learning the near accomplishment of their wishes, were a sure and sacred pledge, that in the hour of trial they would not be found wanting in duty to their country and themselves. But a change of measures, in opposition to the wishes and opinions of all the officers, was adopted by the general. The plan of attacking Malden was abandoned, and instead of acting offensively, we broke up our camp, evacuated Canada, and recrossed the river in the night, without even the shadow of an enemy to injure us. We left to the tender mercy of the enemy, the miserable Canadians who had joined us, and the protection we afforded them was but a passport of vengeance. This fatal and unaccountable step dispirited the troops, and destroyed the little confidence which a series of timid, irresolute and indecisive measures had left in the commanding officer.

About the 10th of August, the enemy received a reinforcement of four hundred men. On the 12th, the commanding officers of three of the regiments (the fourth was absent) were informed through a medium which admitted of no doubt, that the general had stated, that a capitulation would be necessary. They on the same day addressed to Governor Meigs, of Ohio, a letter, of which the following is an extract:

"Believe all the bearer will tell you. Believe it, however it may astonish you, as much as if told by one of us. Even a c——— is talked of by the ——— The bearer will fill the vacancy."

The doubtful fate of this letter rendered it necessary to use circumspection in its details, and therefore the blanks were left. The word "capitulation" will fill the first, and "commanding general" the other. As no enemy was near us, and as the superiority of our force was manifest, we could see no necessity for capitulating, nor any propriety in alluding to it. We therefore determined in the last resort to incur the responsibility of divesting the general of his command. This plan was eventually prevented by two of the commanding officers of regiments being ordered upon detachments.

On the 13th, the British took a position opposite to Detroit, and began to throw up works. During that and the two following days, they pursued their object without interruption, and established a battery for two 18 pounders and an 8 inch howitzer. About sunset on the evening of the 14th, a detachment of 350 men, from the regiments commanded by Colonel McArthur and myself, was ordered to march to the river Raisin, to escort the provisions, which had some time remained there protected by a party under the command of Captain Brush.

On Saturday, the 15th, about 1 o'clock, a flag of truce arrived from Sandwich, bearing a summons from General Brock, for the surrender of the town and Fort of Detroit, stating he could no longer restrain the fury of the savages. To this an immediate and spirited refusal was returned. About 4 o'clock their batteries began to play upon the town. The fire was returned and continued without interruption and with little effect till dark—their shells were thrown till 11 o'clock.

At daylight the firing on both sides recommenced; about the same time the enemy began to land troops at the Spring Wells, three miles below Detroit, protected by two of their armed vessels. Between 6 and 7 o'clock they had effected their landing, and immediately took up their line of march; they moved in a close column of platoons, twelve in front, upon the bank of the river.

The 4th regiment was stationed in the fort; the Ohio volunteers and a part of the Michigan militia, behind some pickets, in a situation in which the whole flank of the enemy would have been exposed. The residue of the Michigan militia were in the upper part of the town to resist the incursions of the savages. Two 24 pounders loaded with grape shot were posted on a commanding eminence, ready to sweep the advancing column. In this situation, the superiority of our position was apparent, and our troops, in the eager expectation of victory, awaited the approach of the enemy. Not a sigh of discontent broke upon the ear; not a look of cowardice met the eye. Every man expected a proud day for his country, and each was anxious that his individual exertion should contribute to the general result.

When the head of their column arrived within about five hundred yards of our line, orders were received from General Hull for the whole to retreat to the fort, and for the twenty-four pounders not to open upon the enemy. One universal burst of indignation was apparent upon the receipt of this order. Those, whose conviction was the deliberate result of a dispassionate examination of passing events, saw the folly and impropriety of crowding 1100 men into a little work, which 300 could fully man, and into which the shot and shells of the enemy were continually falling. The fort was in this manner filled; the men were directed to stack their arms, and scarcely was an opportunity afforded of moving. Shortly after a white flag was hung out upon the walls. A British officer rode up to enquire the cause. A communication passed between the commanding generals, which ended in the capitulation submitted to you. In entering into this capitulation, the general took counsel from his own feelings only. Not an officer was consulted. Not one anticipated a surrender till he saw the white flag displayed. Even the women were indignant at so shameful a degradation of the American character, and all felt as they should have felt, but he who held in his hands the reins of authority.

Our morning report of that morning made our effective men present fit for duty 1060, without including the detachment before alluded to, and without including 300 of the Michigan militia on duty. About dark on Sunday evening the detachment sent to escort the provisions received orders from General

Hull to return with as much expedition as possible. About ten o'clock the next day they arrived within sight of Detroit. Had a firing been heard, or any resistance visible, they would have immediately advanced and attacked the rear of the enemy. The situation in which this detachment was placed, although the result of accident, was the best for annoying the enemy and cutting off his retreat that could have been selected. With his raw troops enclosed between two fires and no hopes of succor, it is hazarding little to say, that very few would have escaped.

I have been informed by Colonel Findley, who saw the return of the quarter master general the day after the surrender, that their whole force of every description, white, red and black, was 1030. They had twenty-nine platoons, twelve in a platoon, of men dressed in uniform. Many of these were evidently Canadian militia. The rest of their militia increased their white force to about seven hundred men.

The number of their Indians could not be ascertained with any degree of precision; not many were visible. And in the event of an attack upon the town and fort, it was a species of force which could have afforded no material advantage to the enemy.

In endeavoring to appreciate the motives and to investigate the causes which led to an event so unexpected and dishonorable, it is impossible to find any solution in the relative strength of the contending parties, or in the measures of resistance in our power. That we were far superior to the enemy; that upon any ordinary principles of calculation, we could have defeated them, the wounded and indignant feelings of every man there will testify.

A few days before the surrender, I was informed by General Hull, we had 400 rounds of 24 pound shot fixed, and about 100,000 cartridges made. We surrendered with the fort 40 barrels of powder and 2500 stand of arms.

The state of our provisions has not been generally understood. On the day of the surrender we had fifteen days of provisions of every kind on hand. Of meat there was plenty in the country, and arrangements had been made for purchasing and grinding the flour. It was calculated we could readily procure three months' provisions, independent of 150 barrels of flour, and 1300 head of cattle which had been forwarded from the state of Ohio, which remained at the river Raisin under Captain Brush, within reach of the army.

But had we been totally destitute of provisions, our duty and our interest undoubtedly was to fight. The enemy invited us to meet him in the field.

By defeating him the whole country would have been open to us, and the object of our expedition gloriously and successfully obtained. If we had been defeated we had nothing to do but to retreat to the fort, and make the best defense which circumstances and our situation rendered practicable. But basely to surrender without firing a gun—tamely to submit without raising a bayonet—disgracefully to pass in review before an enemy as inferior in the quality as in the number of his forces, were circumstances, which excited feelings of indignation more easily felt than described. To see the whole of our men flushed with the hope of victory, eagerly awaiting the approaching contest; to see them afterwards dispirited, hopeless and desponding, at least 500 shedding tears, because they were not allowed to meet their country's foe, and to fight their country's battles, excited sensations, which no American has ever before had cause to feel, and which, I trust in God, will never again be felt, while one man remains to defend the standard of the union.

I am expressly authorized to state, that Colonel McArthur and Colonel Findley, and Lieutenant Colonel Miller, view this transaction in the light which I do. They know and feel, that no circumstance in our situation, none in that of the enemy, can excuse a capitulation so dishonorable and unjustifiable. This too is the universal sentiment among the troops; and I shall be surprised to learn, that there is one man, who thinks it was necessary to sheath his sword, or lay down his musket.

I was informed by general Hull the morning after the capitulation, that the British forces consisted of 1800 regulars, and that he surrendered to prevent the effusion of human blood. That he magnified their regular force nearly five fold, there can be no doubt.

Whether the philanthropic reason assigned by him is a sufficient justification for surrendering a fortified town, an army and a territory, is for the government to determine. Confident I am, that had the courage and conduct of the general been equal to the spirit and zeal of the troops, the event would have been as brilliant and successful as it now is disastrous and dishonorable.

I have the honor to be yours, &c.,

LEWIS CASS.

MICHIGAN IN 1818

Estwick Evans made an extensive
tour of the western portion of
the United States (that is the
present Midwest) during 1818.
He published a fine description
of his tour.  The portion which
follows indicates his view of
the beauties of Michigan as well
as a detailed description of
early Detroit.

Source: Estwick Evans.  A Predestrious Tour of Four
Thousand Miles, Through the Western States and Terri-
tories, During the Winter and Spring of 1818.  in
Reuben Gold Thwaites, ed.  Early Western Travels 1748-
1846.  Cleveland, Ohio: The Arthur H. Clarke Company,
1904, vol. 8.

For twenty miles west of this river there are some
rises of land, the soil of which is light, and the growth
of timber upon them is principally white oak.  In travelling this distance I crossed several creeks, with much
difficulty and hazard.  Up and down the bank of one of
them I marched for hours before I could find a single
tree or log to float upon.  Just before reaching this creek
a bear crossed my path; but having no dogs I could not
overtake him.

Soon after leaving the last mentioned creek, [108] arrived at another, which furnished more means of crossing,
but in the employment of which there was the greatest
peril.  A tree lay part of the way across the channel of the
creek with its top towards me; but being very large its
trunk had sunk far below the surface of the current, so
that I could walk only on its crooked branches.  Having
my gun too, I could employ but one hand in supporting
myself, and sometimes could reach no limb for the employment even of that.  After crossing a part of the channel, I found the large end of the tree several feet below the
surface of the water; and it was disposed to sink further.
At the distance of several feet from the end of it was a
high stump; and from this to the shore there was a space
of water a few feet in depth.  I could take no other course
than to note the direction and extent of the body of the
tree, walk quickly to its end, spring to the stump, and
from that to the shore.  I effected my object; but was
never more sensible of the protecting hand of Providence.
The water of the creek was exceedingly cold, and the chill
of evening was approaching.

It was now the 17th of March, the ground was frozen,
and the travelling very rough and painful.  In the fore-

noon I passed the Bay Settlement.[60]  This place contains several scattering houses, which are occupied principally by French people; and the aspect of the whole country is that of an illimitable marsh.  Some parts of this tract of prairie are too wet for cultivation.  A few miles east of the Bay there are several rises of land, the soil of which is light and well adapted to the cultivation of wheat.

Towards evening I reached the River Raisin.  At the distance of a few miles east of it, I entered the Military Road, of which the public papers have spoken, and which leads to the old roads in the vicinity of Detroit.[61]  This road is cut through a perfect wilderness [109] of a large growth of timber.  It is very wide, and entirely free from stumps.  The plan of it, and the manner in which the work has been executed, speak favourably of the judgment and fidelity of the military department.

The travelling on this road is, in the spring of the year, very heavy; and a person on foot is much annoyed by the sharp points of bushes which are concealed by the mud.

At the commencement of the road the country becomes rather elevated, is highly fertile, is covered with a superb growth of timber, and is intersected with streams well calculated for mills.

On the River Raisin stands Frenchtown, an ancient and considerable settlement.[62]  The inhabitants on the river

---

[60] This was probably the village at the mouth of Otter Creek, forty-two miles southwest of Detroit.  The land had been purchased from the Indians and settlement begun in 1794.— ED.

[61] This road, begun under the direction of the secretary of war, May, 1816 was built by soldiers stationed at Detroit.  By November, 1818, seventy miles had been completed.  It was eighty feet wide and contained over sixty causeways and many bridges.— ED.

[62] In 1784 a small body of French Canadians purchased land from the Indians and settled at the mouth of Raisin River, forty miles south of Detroit.  They traded in furs with the agents of the North West Company.  In 1812 the village contained about forty-five French families and a few Americans.  It has now been incorporated in the city of Monroe.— ED.

are principally French; but the American population is rapidly increasing. The soil here is of an excellent quality, and in high repute. The river, at the settlement, is about sixty rods wide, and it is navigable to Lake Erie, a distance of about twelve miles. The river has been explored for about seventy miles above Frenchtown; and beyond this distance the country is but little known. The land above the settlement is said to be even better than in its immediate vicinity. The name of the river comports well with the nature of the soil; it may be rendered, in English, river of grapes.

I approached this river with a light step and a heavy heart. Hundreds of my gallant countrymen had there fallen victims to British barbarity. Who has heard without horror, of the massacre at the River Raisin![63] When I arrived at this bloody field, the snow had left the hillocks, and the grass began to vegetate upon the soldier's grave. The sun was setting in sadness, and seemed not yet to have left off his weeds. The wind from the north, crossing [110] the icy vales, rebuked the unconscious spring; and the floating ice, striking against the banks of the river, spake of the warrior souls, pressing for waftage across the gulph of death.

In speaking of our too general employment of militia, I suggested, that in another place I should offer some reflections upon the subject of war.

Nothing but the influence of example, and the ability of

---

[63] General Winchester, having reached the Maumee Rapids, did not wait for the remainder of the army under Harrison, but proceeded to Frenchtown, although his men had little ammunition and the town was unprotected, save for a line of pickets. Proctor, the British general, crossed from Malden and attacked him, January 22, 1813. A panic seizing one portion of the army they fled to the woods where they were overtaken and most of them scalped by the Indians; the militia at the same time surrendering to Proctor. Without providing sufficient protection for the wounded left at Frenchtown, this general hastened back to Canada, and the following morning a horde of painted savages broke into the town and shot and scalped the helpless prisoners.— ED.

the human mind readily to accustom itself to crime and
carnage, prevents us from being shocked by sanguinary
contests between civilized communities.   How astonish-
ing is it, that nations, acquainted with the feelings and
principles of humanity, instructed by the precepts and example of the Prince of Peace, and living in the hopes of
Heaven, should send armies into the field to butcher each
other!  The practice is indeed a disgrace to human nature; and the mournful consequences of it must make the
Angels weep.  How often has the hostile foot suddenly
assailed the ear of apprehension!  How often has war
driven man from his home, and blasted forever his plans
of domestic happiness!  How often is the wife called upon
to mourn her husband slain!— The father his son, the
pride and the glory of his old age!— The son his father,
the instructor and the guide of his youth!— The brother,
his brother of love!— And the maiden, the blooming
youth,— the secret joy of her soul!

A state of war is demoralizing in many points of view.
It opens a wide door to selfish ambition,— to intrigue,
avarice, and to all their concomitant crimes.  A habit of
engaging in war is very soon acquired; and then the feelings, and pecuniary interests of a considerable portion of
the community, renders, to them, such a state desirable.
Under such a state of things, the defence of national liberty is often the insincere apology for invasion; and the
splendour [111] of military parade, captivating the heart,
darkens the understanding, and silences the voice of conscience.  The true nature of freedom is here overlooked;
passion supplies the place of reason; and false glory is
substituted for national respectability.  Upon these
grounds, the eclat of military achievements undermines
the virtue of the state, and military tyranny usurps the
place of rational government.

The evil effects of war are incalculable.  They con-

tinue to operate for ages, and materially affect the ultimate destinies of nations. War, however, is sometimes
necessary: but self defence,— in the largest sense of the
phrase; self defence, both at home and on Nature's Com-
mons;— self defence directly and indirectly, is the only
ground upon which it should be waged. Here Heaven
will always smile, and freemen always conquer.

On the 18th and 19th of March I passed the battle
grounds of Brownstown and Magagua.⁶⁴ Near the former place Major Vanhorn, commanding a detachment of
one hundred and fifty men, was suddenly attacked, on all
sides, by British regulars and Indians. The Americans
made a spirited resistance, and after suffering severely
effected a retreat. Soon after this affair another detachment, under Lieutenant Colonel Miller, consisting of three
hundred of the veteran 4th regiment, and also about two
hundred militia, were sent to accomplish the object of Vanhorn's march, which was to support Capt. Brush, who
was encamped at the River Raisin, and who was destined
for Detroit with provisions for our army then in possession
of Sandwich. The enemy anticipating another attempt
to accomplish the object, immediately obtained reinforcements, and lay in ambush near the former battle ground.
The Indians were commanded by Tecumseh; and the
combined forces amounted to about seven hundred and
fifty men.

[112] Colonel Miller, although he proceeded with caution, experienced a sudden attack. Perhaps there never
was one more furious; or the resistance to which evinced
in a greater degree the characteristic union and firmness
of disciplined troops.

---

⁶⁴ Brownstown is situated on the Huron River, twenty-five miles south of
Detroit; Magagua (Monguagon) is about twenty miles south of Detroit. The
engagement at the former place occurred August 5; at the latter, August 9,
1812.— ED.

On the right of the Americans there was a dark wood, and on their left was a small prairie across which was an eminence covered with trees and bushes. In the wood, on the right, the Indians lay in ambush, with a breast-work between them and the Americans. On the small height, on the left, there was stationed a detachment of Indians; and the British regulars occupied other favour-able positions. The onset was tremendous. The veteran Miller immediately extended his lines, to avoid being out-flanked, ordered a detachment to dislodge the enemy on his left, opened a brisk fire upon the main body of the assailants, and then drove them at the point of the bayonet. At the same time, the enemy was driven from the height in a most prompt and gallant manner. The British reg-ulars retreated; but the Indians still obstinately contended from behind the scattering trees. The regulars, in the mean time, were rallied; and the battle became more general, and more equally maintained. At this eventful moment, the mighty, yet cheering voice of the intrepid Miller, like the roar of a torrent echoing from a thousand hills, inspired with a new impulse his faithful,— generous troops.— In one moment the victory was ours. Early in the engagement, the veteran Colonel was, accidentally, thrown from his horse; and some suppose, that they can still see upon the ground the impression of his gigantic form.

In examining this interesting battle-ground, I found, by the numerous scars on the trees under which the Amer-icans fought, that the enemy made a great many random shot. It is to be presumed, [113] that soldiers generally fire too high, especially when the object is at a considerable distance; not considering that a ball, in its passage, de-scribes a circular line. Every soldier should be acquainted with the most simple principles of enginery; and he should practice upon those principles, for the purpose of ascertaining their relative influence upon the character of his piece. General Wayne seemed to be aware that soldiers are apt to fire too high. He was often heard to say to his troops, in battle:—"Shin them my brave boys!— shin them!"

In passing the battle-grounds all was silence. Not a leaf was in motion. The misty air seemed conscious that here was the place of graves; and no sound was heard but the footsteps of the stranger who had come to rejoice and to mourn.

Before leaving these interesting, yet melancholy scenes, I may add, that where one is acquainted with the particulars of an engagement, he can view, with much gratification, the positions which the parties occupied, and draw, from their influences upon the result, important lessons equal to those of actual experience.

From the River Raisin to Brownstown the land is highly valuable, and presents some fine scites for farms. The soil is rugged and rich, the timber upon it lofty and elegant, and the streams remarkably well calculated for manufacturing purposes. In viewing these fine tracts I could not but pity those poor fellows whom I have often seen settled upon a barren and rocky soil, scarcely fit for the pasturage of sheep. Unacquainted with the quality of land, and yet devoted to the employment of agriculture, they still cleave to their possessions, which instead of enriching them, will break down their constitutions with labour, and keep them poor all their days. Such persons, however, need not leave the land of [114] their birth and the society of their friends. Let them still employ their industry at home; not upon a less thankless soil.

From Brownstown to Detroit the land is diversified with small meadows and fertile eminences. Here there is a

beautiful view of the river Detroit.   The rises of land consist of a rich black mould, upon a limestone bottom.   At
the foot of them there are fine springs, and on their summits a good growth of hard wood.

The day after leaving Magagua I arrived at Detroit, to
which place I had long looked for that rest and those comforts, which would enable me to make new exertions.   In
marching to this place I was constantly employed, with
the exception of one day, for seven weeks.   The distance
from New-Hampshire to Detroit, by the rout which I took,
is about one thousand miles.   Ere I reached the city my
clothes became much torn, and in going through the
bushes my eyes were greatly injured.   Within one hundred miles east of Detroit, I crossed upwards of thirty
rivers and creeks.

The prospect in approaching this place is picturesque
and interesting.   At the distance of several miles, the
traveller, in moving along the western bank of the river,
sees several large buildings, and several wind-mills in the
town of Sandwich.   This place is very considerable, and
is situated on the Canada side of the river, opposite Detroit.   The general appearance of this part of the country
is truly European.

The city of Detroit is very beautifully situated.[65]   Its
principal street and buildings are upon a bend of the river,
of a mile or two in length, and they occupy the whole extent of it.   The bend forms a semi-circle, and the banks
of it are gently sloping.   The houses and stores are near
the summit of the bank, [115] and the slopes form pleasant
grounds for gardening.   The streets intersect each other
at right angles, and the situation is calculated for a large
and elegant city.   The Fort and Cantonment lie about

[65] For the early history of Detroit, see Croghan's *Journals*, volume i of our
series, note 18.— ED.

forty rods west of the main street. From this street a
spacious gate opens to them, and at a little distance from
it, the road forks and leads to them respectively. The
contrast between the numerous white buildings in both of
these places, and the green grass contiguous to and around
them is very pleasant. A stranger, in visiting the Fort
and Cantonment, is agreeably impressed with the neat-
ness of their appearance, and with the order and discipline
which are maintained there among the troops. The
apartments of the officers too present a studious and scientific aspect; and seem to warrant the idea, that in the
officers of our army are united the character of the well
informed gentleman, and intrepid soldier. This military
post is a very important and responsible station; and the
government has made for it a very judicious selection of
officers. Several of these officers are of the veteran 4th
regiment; and others of them have seen the darkened sky
red-hot with battle.

On the evening of my arrival at Detroit, I addressed the
following note to Governor Cass: "A gentleman from
New-Hampshire wishes for the privilege of introducing
himself to Governor Cass. He is upon a pedestrious tour,
and therefore trusts, that the roughness of his garb will not
preclude him from the honour of an interview. March
20th, 1818." The Governor replied with his compliments
and with the request that I would call upon him the next
morning at 9 o'clock. At the time appointed I waited
upon him, and was received with that unaffected friend-
liness and manner, which so well comports with the insti-
tutions of the country.

[116] Governor Cass,[66] who is the Supreme Executive
magistrate of the Michigan Territory, resides just below

[66] Lewis Cass was governor of Michigan from 1814 to 1831.— ED.

the Cantonment; and General Macomb [47] occupies an
elegant brick house, erected by General Hull, situated at
the upper end of the street.   The former is remarkably
well calculated for the Governor of a frontier Territory:
in him are united the civilian and the warrior.   Governor
Cass lives in an unostentatious style; his aspect evinces
benevolence; his disposition is social, and his manners are
plain.

The style in which General Macomb lives is at once elegant and becoming.  His military reputation is well
known; and in private life he is conspicuous for affabil-
ity, politeness and attention to strangers.

Soon after entering Detroit, I met with a trifling incident,
which interested me by exciting my curiosity.   Among a
crowd of gazers here, I saw a face which I remembered to
have known a great while before; but where, I could not
tell.  How astonishingly impressive is the expression of
the human countenance!   The next day the man passed
the Hotel where I sojourned, and I took the liberty to in-
vite him in.   Twenty years had elapsed since I had last
seen him; and then we were mere children, pronouncing
in the same class our A, B, C.

A considerable part of the population of Detroit are
French; but the number of Americans there, is daily increasing, and will soon become very numerous.   The Government warehouse here is very large, and the Government wharf is long and commodious.   There are several
other wharves at Detroit, and the vessels lying at them

---

[47] Alexander Macomb (1782-1841) was a lieutenant-colonel in the regular
army at the outbreak of the War of 1812-15.  Having served on the Niagara
frontier during 1813, he commanded the regular troops at the battle of Platts-
burg (September, 1814), and for his bravery was made a major-general and received a gold medal from Congress.  Upon the death of General Brown in
1828, he was appointed commander-in-chief of the army.— ED.

make a pleasant appearance. From the lower part of the town the view, up the river, is remarkably fine. Here one may see, for the distance of four miles, a beautiful expanse of water, several islands almost lost to vision, and near [117] them, on a point of land, several large wind-mills. The river itself yields to none in point of utility and beauty. Opposite to Detroit it is about one mile wide, and its current moves about three miles an hour. The whole length of the river is thirty miles; and from Detroit to Lake St. Clair the distance is nine miles.

In Detroit there is much good society; and hospitality is a conspicuous trait in the character of the people. The Lyceum established here is patronized by the principal men in the place; and those who take a part in its discussions display extensive information, much correct reasoning, and no little eloquence. There is also an Academy in this place; and it is superintended by the learned Mr. Monteith. In time, this city will become conspicuous for its literature, and for the propriety of its customs and manners. In relation to politics, it will take, in some respects, a new course; and in this particular be an example worthy of imitation. In point too of municipal regulation and statutary rule, the Michigan Territory will be eminently correct. There is no state or territory in the union, which merits so much attention on the part of the General Government as the Michigan Territory. In the vicinity of Detroit there is, for the distance of thirty miles, only the width of the river of this name between the United States and Upper Canada; and above Lake St. Clair, there is between the two countries only the width of the river St. Clair for the distance of forty miles. It will be of great consequence, in a national point of view, to have the systems of education, laws, customs, and manners, of the Territory such as to outweigh the counter influence of those of the British in its neighbourhood.  As to the population of this territory, the General Government will do well to afford every facility and encouragement to [118] its increase.  By increasing the strength of our frontier settlements, we shall lessen the influence of the British Government over the savages of the west, and be able to meet their incursions more promptly, and with greater effect.

At Detroit there is a theatre; and it is under the exclusive management of the military officers stationed there. These gentlemen, actuated by liberal and polished views, have erected a stage for the gratuitous instruction and amusement of the public.  The scenery of the stage is executed with an appropriate taste, the dramatic pieces are selected with judgment and delicacy, and the performances are quite equal to any in the country.  Indeed the officers of our army, at Detroit, possess much genius and erudition; and the correctness of their conduct, in point of morals and manners, entitle them to much praise.

The state of agriculture in the Michigan Territory is far from flourishing.  In the immediate vicinity of Detroit it is deplorable.  The French have no ambition to excel in this honourable and profitable calling.  There is here, however, every thing to encourage an active husbandman. The soil is fertile and the climate perfectly congenial to the growth of New-England productions.  A yankee farmer, carrying with him to this place his knowledge of agriculture, and his industry, might soon acquire a very handsome estate.  The market for country produce in Detroit is always high; and large sums of money are annually paid there for provisions, which are transported across the lake from the upper parts of the states of New-York, Pennsylvania, and Ohio.

The inhabitants of Detroit, wishing to keep their money in circulation among themselves, and also wishing to see their own agriculture improving, [119] would afford great encouragement to farmers who should settle in their vicinity. Here too all mechanical trades would be promptly patronized. Various articles of American manufacture are sent to this place from the city of New-York, and meet here a market affording great profits. Joiners, brick makers, shoe makers, and almost all other mechanics would here find ample patronage. Day labourers too, would obtain here ready employment and good wages. I may add, that lumber and wood are remarkably high in this city; and that wood sellers and lumber dealers might here realize from these occupations very handsome profits.

I deem it my duty to express a high opinion of the Michigan Territory, because facts warrant such a course, and it is important that those of my fellow citizens, who may be disposed to emigrate to the west, should possess every information upon the subject. No one need suppose my declarations to be those of a land speculator. I have not the most remote relation to such business, and never expect to have.

In travelling more than four thousand miles, in the western parts of the United States, I met no tract of country which, upon the whole, impressed my mind so favourably as the Michigan Territory. Erroneous ideas have heretofore been entertained respecting this territory. Indeed it has, until lately, been viewed as scarcely within the jurisdiction of the United States. Even some late geographers seem to have collected no other information respecting it, than what had been written by their ancient predecessors. Some of this information, especially as it respects Detroit, does not apply to the present times.

The soil of this territory is generally fertile, and a considerable proportion of it is very rich. Its [120] climate is delightful; and its situation novel and interesting. As

to the former, it possesses a good medium between our
extreme northern and southern latitudes; and with respect to the latter it is almost encircled by the Lakes Erie,
St. Clair, Huron, and Michigan. New-England fruits
may here be produced in great perfection; and the territory is capable of being rendered a great cider country.
In point of health too, this territory yields to no part of
North America. There is no place in the world more
healthy than the city of Detroit. Consumptions are never
known there.

The situation of this city, although level, is very commanding. On the Ohio the view of the traveller is con-
fined; but here one appears lifted above the adjacent
country, and may survey it as from an eminence.

The Michigan Territory is generally level, but in many
places gently diversified. The growth of timber here is
principally black walnut, sugar maple, elm, sycamore, and
pine. There is not, however, an abundance of the latter.
The streams within this territory are very numerous, and
well calculated for manufactures of every kind; and the
fisheries here are exceedingly valuable. Besides vast
quantities of many other kinds of fish, caught in the waters
within and contiguous to this territory, during the spring
and summer season, thousands of barrels of white fish
are taken here in the fall, and prepared for the home and
foreign markets.[68] This species of fish is of the size, and
appearance of the largest shad; but are far more valuable.
Wild fowl of all kinds greatly abound here.

The trade of the Michigan Territory is already very considerable, and it is rapidly increasing. Besides the business transacted between different parts of the territory itself, and with the Indian [121] tribes in the neighbourhood,

[68] Either the common whitefish (*Coregonus clupeiformis*) or the blue fins
(*Coregonus nigripinnis*).— ED.

it transacts considerable business with the upper parts of
the state of New-York, Pennsylvania, and Ohio; and also
with the inhabitants of Upper Canada. Its shipping is
employed on Lake Erie, Huron, and Michigan, either
in the fisheries, in freighting, or in trading along the coast.
In the summer season there is in Detroit a considerable
concourse of strangers, from the states by the way of
Buffalo, who furnish considerable sums as passage money
to the ship owners on Lake Erie; and in the spring of the
year the neighbouring Indians resort thither to dispose of
their furs, and to purchase guns, ammunition, blankets,
and other articles.

Detroit is a central situation for the fur trade in the
North-West;[69] and there is a considerable commercial
connexion between this place and Chicago and Green
Bay.

The establishment of a weighty fur company at Detroit,
would result in much individual and public advantage.
The English, by their extensive fur trade in the north and
west, acquire an influence among the Indians, which similar establishments on our part would completely counter-
act. This influence renders the Indians hostile towards
us, and in the event of a war between this country and
Great Britain, would blend the prejudices of the Englishman with the ferocity of the savage.

The English derive immense profits from the North
American fur trade. The North West company employ
in this business, exclusive of savages, upwards of fifteen
hundred men. The articles for the Indian market are
cheap, and of course the requisite capital for this business
is small.

It was my intention, after spending a few days at De-

---

[69] For an account of the North West Company, consult the preface to Long's
*Voyages*, volume ii of our series, p. 16.— ED.

troit, to pursue my tour through the wilderness, between
the Lakes Huron and Michigan, as far as [122] Michili-
macinac; from thence across the North-West Territory to
the Falls of St. Anthony, and then to trace the Mississippi
to New-Orleans. Whilst at Detroit, however, I concluded
to change, in some measure, my course.

There was evidence of a hostile disposition on the part
of the Indians situated on my proposed route; the season
of the year rendered travelling in this direction almost impracticable; and my views and business would not permit the delay which this last mentioned circumstance
would occasion.

Upon leaving Detroit I crossed Lake Erie in a small
vessel, and arriving at Presque Isle, pursued my course to
New-Orleans, taking in my way all the states and terri-
tories of the west.

It may not be amiss, before I notice my trip across the
Lake, to communicate some facts and reflections respecting the country above Detroit, many of which facts I was
enabled to obtain by my residence there. Ere I speak
upon this subject, however, I will, for a moment, prolong
my stay at this city.

The sufferings of this place during the late war, are
scarcely describable. The apprehension of death is far
more terrible than actual dissolution. After the capitulation of General Hull, Detroit was thronged by Indians, and
they were continually making the most aggravating requi-
sitions. These they enforced by savage threats. There
was not a moment of domestic peace for any one. The
inhabitants did not dare to fasten their doors: for if they
did the Indians would cut them to pieces with their toma-
hawks, and revenge the opposition upon the inmates of
the house. When families were about to sit down to their
tables, the Indians would come in, drive every one out of

the room, and feast themselves. Their constant demand, at every dwelling, was for [123] whiskey; and to grant or refuse it was attended with great danger. If it were granted, intoxication and consequent bloodshed would be the effects; and upon a refusal, the Indians would present their long knives and threaten immediate death.

A lady, who resided at Detroit whilst it was in possession of the British, and who is remarkable for her good sense and intrepidity, related to me the above and many other facts relative to this trying state of things. She said, that upon one occasion several Indians came to her house, and upon their approach it was thought advisable for her husband to conceal himself in the garret. The Indians demanded whiskey of her; and upon being told that there was none in the house, they presented several knives to her breast, and in their rude English called her a liar. Although in momentary expectation of death, she still denied her having whiskey. Her husband, hearing the bustle below came down, and with the assistance of two or three others, who accidentally came that way, drave the Indians from the house. Immediate revenge was anticipated. It was the practice of the Indians, particularly at this time, to resent the smallest opposition. Supported by their civilized patrons, they felt their consequence; and their pride was as easily touched as that of a savageized Englishman. The house of the lady was soon surrounded, and day after day the Indians came to search for her husband; but not being able to find him, the object was, apparently, abandoned.

Immediately after the massacre at the River Raisin, the inhabitants of Detroit were called upon to witness a heart-rending scene. The Indians from this field of carnage were continually arriving at the city, and passing through its streets, with poles laden with reeking scalps.

I am here disposed to make a few remarks relative [124] to the late war.   I know that in so doing I shall incur cen- sure; but I write for those who are too noble to conceal their defeats, and too modest to proclaim their victories. The genius, and energy, and resources of the United States should have accomplished every thing.

I confess that I did not rejoice at the beams of peace. Premature peace does not promote the cause of humanity. We declared war for the defence of essential rights, which had, in the wantonness of power, been repeatedly invaded. In this war we sought indemnity for the past, and security for the future;— that security which punishment extorts from injustice:— that security which the fine and the lash guarantees to honest and peaceable communities.   Did we effect our object ?— Oh no!   Whatever may have been our victories, our defeats were disgraceful.   The admin- istrators of the government were deficient in information, in system, and in energy.   They sought an effect without an adequate cause;  and the people sacrificed the glory of the country to the pride of political competition.   As to the opposition, they pursued false morals until they lost sight of true patriotism.

There was virtue enough in the community; but afflic- tion was necessary to raise it from the ruins of thoughtless and passionate rivalry.   We were upon the eve of humil- iation,— the eve of new, and omnipotent moral impulse, when peace unexpectedly presented herself.   Not the peace which the victor magnanimously gives to the humbled foe, but that peace which misguided apprehension yields to the dark calculations of policy.   The British Lion ceased to roar, and instead of contending until we had pared his princely paws, we were ready to forgive and to embrace him.   Our own Eagle despised us; and with a fearless, anxious eye, and ruffled plume, [125] retired to the elevated

and gloomy promontory of her glory and her disappoint-
ment.

It is the general opinion at Detroit, that Hull was
prompted to surrender the place, not by bribery, but by
cowardice. Could he have seen the dreadful and humiliat-
ing consequences which actually arose from this base
and unpardonable step, the suggestions of conscience
would have controuled his apprehensions, and his brave
men would not have been deprived of their fame. Inde-
scribable must be the feelings of patriotism and courage,
when official cowardice yields them to a foe, whom their
hearts have already conquered. The brave man regards
his friends and his country a thousand times more than
himself; and he would court a hundred deaths rather than
wound their feelings, or forfeit their love. In the hour of
danger, when the national flag is assailed, his soul tells
him that his countrymen will hear of this, and he dedicates
himself to battle, to glory, and to death! But I am sensible that there is a higher principle: the man who fears no
evil so much as self-reproach, will always do his duty.-

Immediately upon the capitulation of Hull, a Yankee
soldier of the 4th regiment thought it high time for him
to take care of himself; and he immediately devised a plan
by which he hoped to outwit General Brock. The soldier
secretly left the fort, went to a barber and had his hair
and whiskers closely shaved; and then obtained from a
tailor such garments as were most fashionable for traders.
After remaining about the city for a few days, this citizen-
soldier applied to the British General for the necessary
passes, stating that he had come to Detroit for the purposes of trade, &c. The General kindly referred him to
the proper officer, his passes were promptly prepared, and
he returned to his friends.

[126] I will now commence my proposed excursion above Detroit.

The strait called the river Detroit becomes enlarged just above Hog Island,[70] and forms Lake St. Clair. This lake is about twenty-five miles in length. Its depth is inconsiderable. The principal islands in it are Harsen's, Hay, Peach, and Thompson's. Formerly there were several Indian tribes situated on the western side of this Lake; and the Ontaonais [71] occupied the other side: but the Iroquois, a fierce, bloody, and restless tribe, have long since dispossessed them.

The River St. Clair, between the lake of this name and Lake Huron, receives the waters of the three vast Lakes beyond it. This river is about forty miles long. The bed of the river is strait, contains many islands, and its banks are covered with lofty trees. At the head of this river is Fort St. Clair.[72]

The river Thames enters Lake St. Clair on the Canada side. On this river is situated the Moravian village, where General Harrison routed the British and Indians under Proctor and Tecumseh.[73] On this river too is

---

[70] Hog Island, about three miles above Detroit, was so named by the French in the early years of discovery, because of the number of wild swine found thereon. Near this island occurred the defeat of the Fox Indians in 1712. See *Wisconsin Historical Collections*, xvi, p. 283. This island was purchased by William, father of General Macomb, in 1786.— ED.

[71] For the Ottawa Indians, see Croghan's *Journals*, volume i of our series, note 37.— ED.

[72] This unimportant post was established (1765) and commanded by Patrick Sinclair, a British army officer, who also purchased a large tract of land along the river. Both fort and river were for a long time called Sinclair, and as late as 1807 are so given in an Indian treaty drawn up by Governor Hull. See *State Papers, Indian Affairs*, i, p. 747.— ED.

[73] The battle of the Thames, in which Proctor was put to flight and Tecumseh killed, was fought two miles west of Moraviantown, or about sixty-five miles northeast of Detroit.— ED.

General Simcoe's paper town called London.[74]  Along the banks of the Lake and river St. Clair, the country, generally, is fertile, and pleasingly diversified.  The sugar maple tree abounds here, and here too are elegant forests of pine timber well calculated for the common purposes of building, and also for spars.  I may add, that on the banks of the Thames are villages of the Delawares and Chippewas.[75].  The principal townships of the Six Nations are situated near the greatest source of this river.

Before I leave Lake St. Clair, I must say a word respecting the old veteran of this name.[76]  It is indeed too late to do him justice:— he no longer wants [127] the meat which perisheth.  But we may spread laurels upon his tomb; and soothe the spirit, which, perhaps, even now hovers over its country, and seeks the fame which his merit achieved.  The mass of mankind judge of plans, and of their execution, not by their abstract wisdom, or energy, but by their results.  Many a man, however, gains a victory by a blunder, and experiences defeat through the instrumentality of his wisdom.  Accident often settles the question; and we may presume, that sometimes it is emphatically the will of Heaven, that the strongest and wisest party should be overcome.

General St. Clair devoted his whole life to the art of

[74] In 1793 Governor Simcoe made a trip to Detroit, and selected the present site of London for the capital of Upper Canada.  However, the surrender of Detroit (1796), in accordance with Jay's Treaty, rendered such a plan impracticable, and York was chosen capital instead.  London, situated on the Thames one hundred and ten miles northeast of Detroit, was laid out in 1826 and incorporated in 1840.— ED.

[75] For the Delaware and Chippewa Indians, see Post's *Journals*, volume i of our series, note 57; Long's *Voyages*, volume ii of our series, note 42.— ED.

[76] For a brief biography of General Arthur St. Clair, see F. A. Michaux's *Travels*, volume iii of our series, note 33.  Evans would seem to imply that the lake and river were named for this officer.  The name was assigned by La Salle's expedition in 1679.  See Hennepin, *A New Discovery* (Thwaites's ed., Chicago, 1903), pp. 59, 108.— ED.

war. He was a scientific man, a man of talents, and
always brave. His heart was formed for friendship, and
his manners were interesting. In many battles he pre-
vailed. In 1791 he was defeated.— So was Braddock, so
was Harmer. Indian warfare is full of stratagem and
terror. Troops will not always stand this test, and one
man cannot effect every thing. General St. Clair had to
contend with even more formidable enemies:— with misfortune,— with reproach,— with the ingratitude of his
country. He retired from an ignorant and uncharitable
world to his favourite Ridge.— Here he died. Who
would not shun the thronged and splendid path of the
successful warrior, to bend over the lonely grave of the
venerable St. Clair!

Lake Huron is, excepting Lake Superior, the largest
collection of fresh water known to civilized man. Including the coasts of its bays its circumference is upwards of
one thousand miles. Its islands are very numerous.
The names of some of them are La Crose, Traverse, White-
wood, Michilimackinac, Prince William, St. Joseph, and
Thunder Bay. The island of St. Joseph is upwards of one
hundred miles in circumference, and belongs to the English, who have a company stationed there.[77]

[128] On the American side of Lake Huron, and between it and Lake Michigan the country is a perfect wilderness. The principal Indian tribes situated in this tract
are the Ootewas and Chippewas. The bay of Saguina on
this side of the lake, is eighteen miles in width, and in
length about forty-five miles. Two considerable rivers

[77] The English, upon their surrender of Mackinac in 1796, thinking the
Americans might claim St. Joseph Island, hastened to take possession. A
stockade was erected and subsequently a blockhouse, but the place was not
suited for a military station. In 1815, the buildings were repaired and a garrison established; it was removed, however, to Drummond's Island the following
year. For further information regarding this island, see *Michigan Pioneer
Collections*, xvi, p. 69.— ED.

and several small ones pass into this bay. The Bay of
Thunder lies near the Straits of Michilimackinac, is nine
miles in width and very shallow. Here terrible storms
of thunder and lightning are frequently experienced.

On the Canada side of Lake Huron, from Lake St.
Clair to the river Severn, which passes near Lake Simcoe
and enters the first mentioned Lake, the country is but
little known, and is covered with thick forests. These
forests reach far beyond the Severn, and indeed are separated from the unexplored wilds, which probably extend
to the Pacific Ocean, only by the lakes, rivers, and portages which lie in the track of the British Fur Companies.
The rapids upon these rivers are very numerous. The
lakes too, in this part of the country, are numerous, but
small. The principal houses of the British Fur Companies are established at the Lakes Abitibee, Waratouba,
and Tamiscamine.[78] The North-West Fur Company send
every year from one hundred to one hundred and fifty
canoes, laden with merchandize, to their posts on Lake
Superior. These canoes are made of very light materials,
generally of birch, are 'flat on the bottom, round on the
sides, and sharp at each end. They carry about four tons
each, and are conducted by about ten persons. These
boats generally move from Montreal about the beginning
of May. Before the canoes arrive at their place of destina-
tion, they are repeatedly unladen and carried, together
with their cargoes, across many portages. The course is
toilsome and perilous; but the prospect of [129] gain, and
the habit of enduring fatigue render the employment tol-
erable. The principal food of the navigators is Indian
meal and the fat of bears. In the trade with the Indians,
the beaver skin is the medium of barter. Two beaver

---

[78] For information concerning these lakes, see Long's *Voyages*, volume ii of
our series, pp. 145, 191.— ED.

skins are equal to one otter skin; and ten of the former are
generally allowed for a common gun. Here is a profit of
at least 500 per cent, exclusive of all costs.

Michilimackinac is a small island situated in the upper
part of Lake Huron near the commencement of the strait
which connects this Lake with Lake Michigan.[79] The aspect of the island is elevated and irregular. The fort of
Michilimackinac is situated on this island, near to which
are several stores and dwelling houses. This is a very important post. The strait and also the lakes which it connects abound with fine fish; the principal kinds of which
are herring, white fish, and trout. The Michilimackinac
trout are bred in Lake Michigan, and are celebrated for
their size and excellence; they sometimes weigh sixty or
seventy pounds.

The strait of Michilimackinac is about fifteen miles in
length. The course of its current, into Huron or Michigan, depends upon the winds; and is, therefore, very irregular. At times it is exceedingly rapid.

Lake Michigan is about two hundred and fifty miles in
length. Its breadth is about sixty miles. Including the
curvatures of its bays, its circumference is about nine hundred miles. There are a great many rivers which rise in
the peninsula between this Lake and Lake Huron, and
which pass into the latter. That part of this peninsula
which lies along the south-east of Lake Michigan is but
little known. The names of the principal rivers here are
Marguerite, Grand, Black, and St. Joseph. The latter is
by far the largest, and may be ascended about one hundred [130] and fifty miles. On this river is situated Fort
Joseph.[80]

[79] For the early history of Mackinac, see Thwaites, "Story of Mackinac,"
in *How George Rogers Clark won the Northwest* (Chicago, 1903).— ED.

[80] A brief sketch of Fort St. Joseph is given in Croghan's *Journals*, volume
i of our series, note 85.— ED.

Green Bay, on the western border of Lake Michigan is
about one hundred miles in length; and its breadth, at its
entrance, is about twenty-five miles.   It contains several
islands; and there are in its vicinity tracts of low and wet
ground.   At the bottom of the bay is a little fall,[81] beyond
which is a small lake called Winnebago.   This lake receives Fox river from the west.   At the foot of this bay too,
is a fort,[82] and on the west of lake Winnebago is situated
a village inhabited by Indians of this name.   On the Malhominis river, which flows into Green Bay, is also situated
an Indian village containing various tribes.   The principal of them are the Lake, Pouteoratamis, and Malhominis.[83]   A few families of the Nadonaicks, whose nation
was nearly exterminated by the Iroquois, reside here.   The
Puans once occupied the borders of this bay, and Puans
bay was originally its name.   The Puans were fierce, and
exceedingly hostile to neighbouring tribes.   At length
these tribes combined against them, and their numbers
were greatly diminished.

Lake Michigan and Green Bay form a long point of

[81] Evans probably refers here to the fall five miles from the mouth of Fox
River, at De Pere (French, *Rapides des pères*), so called because it was the site
of a Jesuit Indian mission established in 1669-70.   See *Wisconsin Historical
Collections*, xvi.   Our author in his description omits mention of the Lower
Fox, flowing from Lake Winnebago into Green Bay.— ED.

[82] Fort Howard, named in honor of General Benjamin Howard, formerly
commander in the Western territory, was constructed (1816) a mile above the
mouth of Fox River, when the Americans took possession, after the War of
1812-15.   A French settlement, chiefly on the opposite side of the river at Green
Bay, had existed here since about 1745.— ED.

[83] There were two villages of Winnebago (French Puans) on the lake of that
name: the principal one was situated on Doty's Island, at the mouth of the
lake; the other at the junction of the Upper Fox and the lake, near the water-
works station of the modern Oshkosh.   This latter was familiarly known to the
French voyageurs as Saukière.   The village on the Menominee (Malhominis)
River was, as Evans says, a mixed one, composed principally of the tribe which
gave name to the river.   For these two tribes, see Long's *Voyages*, volume ii of
our series, notes 81, 86.   For the Potawatomi, see Croghan's *Journals*, volume i
of our series, note 84.— ED.

land called Cape Townsand. Between this Lake and
Lake Winnebago are situated the Ootewas. There are
several rivers on the west of the last mentioned lake. One
of these is Chicago river, near to which is Fort Dearborn.[84]
At Chicago the United States have troops stationed.

Would to Heaven, that I could forever forget lake Michigan! Her envious waves have, recently, buried a youth
of noble promise. With melancholy pride I remember,
that whilst at Detroit, I numbered among my friends the
lamented Lieutenant Eveleth. He possessed a genius
peculiarly calculated for the engineer department, to which
he belonged; [131] and by his mild, yet manly deportment,
inspired, even in strangers, both esteem and affection.
His countenance was martial; but with this aspect was
blended a sweetness of expression which is rarely wit-
nessed.—

> "Weep no more," brother soldiers, "weep no more,
> For Lycidas, your sorrow, is not dead,
> Sunk though he be beneath the watery floor;
> So sinks the day star in the ocean bed,
> And yet anon repairs his drooping head,
> And tricks his beams, and with new spangled ore
> Flames in the forehead of the morning sky:
> So Lycidas sunk low, but mounted high,
> Through the dear might of Him who walk'd the wave."

The tract of country lying between Lake Michigan and
Lake Superior is rather sterile. The falls of St. Mary,
situated in the strait between Lakes Huron and Superior,
are mere cascades. In this strait there are several islands.

---

[84] A piece of land six miles square situated on the Chicago River, having
been ceded to the United States by the treaty of Greenville (1795), orders were
issued by the War Department (1803) for the construction of a fort on the
north branch of the river. Fearing a combined English and Indian attack, the
garrison evacuated the fort August 15, 1812; but had proceeded but a little
way, when they were attacked by the Indians and the greater number massacred.
Fort Dearborn was rebuilt in 1816, and garrisoned for several years thereafter.
It was torn down in 1857, and the last of the buildings connected with it were
consumed in the Chicago fire of 1871.— ED.

Below the falls is situated Fort St. Mary.[85]  In this strait
are caught fine fish of many kinds.  The Indian tribes,
who have heretofore occupied, and some of whom still
occupy this part of the country are the Nougua, Outch-
ebous, Maramegs, Achiligonans, Amicours, Missasangues,
Hurons, Nepicrenians, Salteurs, Ontaouais, Amehouest
and Otters.[86]  Many of these tribes are merged in others
of them who have been more powerful, or less unfortunate.
The Iroquois, bloodthirsty and incursive, scattered all
these tribes, and nearly exterminated some of them.  There
is, near the falls of St. Mary, a company of traders, several
houses, a manufactory, mills, &c.  But the vicinity of this
place is a perfect wilderness.

Lake Superior is probably the largest collection of fresh
water in the world.  It is but little known.  Its circumference however, has been ascertained to be about fifteen
hundred miles.  Storms frequently [132] assail it; and a
swell, like that of the ocean, dashes upon the high and ragged rocks of its coasts.  It contains many considerable
islands and bays, and the soil around it is far from being
fertile.  Some of the islands are from fifty to one hundred
miles in length.  There are about forty rivers, which pour
their tribute into this vast lake, some of which are of considerable magnitude.  In the vicinity of the grand portage,[87]
between this lake and the Lake of the Woods, there are
established several trading companies.  Lake Superior is
well stored with fish, the principal kinds of which are
white fish, trout, and sturgeon.  The latter are of a very
superior quality.

[85] For a brief description of Sault Ste. Marie, consult Long's *Voyages,*
volume ii of our series, note 38.— ED.

[86] For these tribes, many of whom are merely clans of the larger tribes, consult *Wisconsin Historical Collections,* xvi, index.— ED.

[87] See Franchère's *Narrative,* volume vi of our series, note 205, for a brief
description of the Grand Portage.— ED.

This lake is remarkable for the pure and pellucid appearance of its water. The fish in it can be seen swimming at a great depth; and the vessels upon it seem to move in air. These effects are, probably, caused, in part, by the peculiar materials of the bed of the lake, and partly by extraordinary evaporation. This last idea sanctions the belief, that in this part of the country the quantity of rain is very great. Some places in the neighbourhood of this Lake are swampy, and some are elevated and fertile.

To the north and west of Lake Superior are several other lakes, the principal of which are the Lake of the Woods, Rainy Lake, Bear Lake, and Red Lake.[88]

Opposite to about the centre of Lake Superior, and on the river Mississippi, are the falls of St. Anthony. This river, above the falls, runs, principally, through Bear and Red Lake; one branch of it, however, runs below them pretty much in the direction of the Missouri River. Both below and above the falls of St. Anthony an almost innumerable number of rivers pour their waters into the Mississippi, some of which are several thousand miles in length. The Missouri is the principal source of [133] the Mississippi, and the latter name ought to be substituted for that of the former. Between the cascades of St. Mary, and the falls last mentioned, lies the North-West Territory.[89]

---

[88] For Lake of the Woods and Rainy Lake, see Franchère's *Narrative*, notes 201, 204.

The maps of Evans's period represent White Bear Lake as the source of the Mississippi, and Red or Mississagan Lake as the origin of Red River of the North. The latter retains its name. The former is probably that now known as Leech Lake.— ED.

[89] Illinois was admitted to the Union in 1818, and the part north of its present boundary was annexed to Michigan Territory. For the various divisions of the Northwest Territory, see Thwaites, "Division of the Northwest," in *How George Rogers Clark won the Northwest.*— ED.

The Indians, in the north and west, are generally fierce
and untameable. They are so attached to the hunter
state, that here they are somewhat industrious; but in
every other occupation they evince great characteristic
indolence. Some of the tribes are politic in all their proceedings; and husband their property and strength.
Others, however, are regardless of the future, and look
only to the present moment. All are degenerating, in a
greater or less degree, and some, through the operation
of ordinary causes, are becoming extinct.

Before I leave these immense waters to return to Detroit,
I may notice, for a moment, the vast inland navigation
which they afford. From the City of New-York to New-
Orleans, by the way of the Lakes, the distance is about
four thousand miles; and yet, without the aid of canals,
the land carriage through this whole route is only about
thirty miles. Such is the wonderful superiority of our
country relative to inland navigation. Owing to this easy
communication between the interior and the sea board,
and to the other advantages of a residence in the west, it
is to be presumed, that in the course of two centuries the
western world will be as populous as the Continent of
Europe. Such are the prospects presented to the politi-
cian in this country, and such the interest which they are
calculated to excite in the breast of the American patriot,
that one, in relation to this subject, would wish to live a
thousand years. Admiration and concern occupy his
mind. He wishes to watch the progress of events; and to
apply, from time to time, the salutary principles of rational
government. Aware of the oscillating nature of popular [134] sentiment, he fears that in some unfortunate moment the waves of popular feeling will be agitated, and
that they will continue to dash even after the cause of their
vexation shall have been forgotten.— He realizes, that in

proportion to the extent of national territory, viewed in connection with the increase of population, the accumulation of wealth, the progress of arts, the habits of refinement, the corruptions of luxury, and lastly, with the dregs of that spirit of independence, which, in its purest essence, blends charity with suspicion, and forbearance with energy; but, in its deterioration, substitutes for these, a contracted jealousy, and a blind resentment:— he realizes, that in proportion to the extent of national territory, viewed in relation to these circumstances, will be the horrors of political concussion, and the miseries of consequent anarchy or despotism.   Such are the effects, which are to be apprehended from the rapid and ultimate increase of the United States, that the American patriot, in view of her prosperity and of his own dissolution, may well exclaim, Oh, save my country!

It is with nations as with individuals; adversity is equally requisite for both.   This is the only school where true wisdom can be acquired, and where the native luxuriance of the heart can meet with due restraints.— May Heaven guide our destinies by his chastening mercy!

I now suppose myself at Detroit, and about to leave it for the purpose of crossing Lake Erie.   I speak not in vanity, but to do justice to the hospitality of this city:   I arrived here an entire stranger, and left the place surrounded by friends.   How grateful to the traveller, worn down by fatigue, is the hand of friendship and the smile of approbation!   Upon leaving the Government wharf, I felt more than I should be willing to express: — The world do [135] not understand the language of the heart. I consider myself under particular obligations to A. G. W. Esquire.   He voluntarily sought my acquaintance, and in the most interesting manner convinced me of his regard. This gentleman is conspicuous for his independence and literary attainments; but his greatest characteristic is native modesty.

Whilst at Detroit, I was much interested and amused by the conduct of an Indian; both by the principles upon which he acted, and the manner with which he displayed them. One morning, whilst conversing with my friend Doctor W. in came an Indian, and putting a finger to his mouth said, with a patient aspect and in a plaintive tone, "very sick." The poor fellow had been suffering much from the tooth ache, and he wished to have it extracted. He sat down, and placing his hands together, and interlocking his fingers he evinced, during the operation, much stoicism mingled with an interesting resignation. After the tooth was removed, he asked for whiskey; and immediately upon drinking it gravely marched off, leaving his tooth as the only compensation for the whiskey and surgical aid.

In going down the river Detroit, I was so happy as to have the society of General Macomb, Major M. Capt. W. and Lieut. B.

The river, a mile below the city, is much wider than it is opposite to that place; and a little further down there is a narrow and marshy island about four miles in length. Here we landed and refreshed ourselves from the General's provision baskets. Upon this island we found an almost innumerable number of ducks; they were heard in the grass in every direction. Vast flocks of wild fowl are almost continually swimming in the river Detroit.

Soon after leaving this island we arrived at Grose Isle.[90] The latter divides the river into two channels. [136] Its

---

[90] Grosse Isle, nine miles in length and about a mile in width, was purchased from the Indians in 1776 by William Macomb; it extends to the mouth of Detroit Strait.— ED.

soil appears to be good, and its timber valuable.  Upon
this island, situated about three miles above Malden, there
is a small fort in which the United States have stationed a
few troops.  The situation is very pleasant; and as a military post, is of consequence.  A little below this place is a
beautiful summer residence belonging to General Macomb,
and which, I believe, is called St. Helena.  The outlet to
Lake Erie, between Malden and the adjoining land, is
very narrow.  Malden itself is a wretched looking place.
It appears, indeed, like a scalp shop.  One store, a warehouse, and a few small buildings constitute the whole of
this celebrated position.  I saw no inhabitants there excepting two or three crippled Indians.

After remaining one night at Grose Isle, I proceeded to
Malden, and from thence entered the lake.  During the
night the wind was high, and we run back a considerable
way to avoid several islands called the Sisters.  Towards
morning, the wind being fair, we continued our course.
At day light we experienced a gale of wind, and run for
Put-in-Bay.  Our Captain was a very experienced seaman, and perfectly understood the navigation of the lake;
but having got among a cluster of little islands, situated
near the bay, he was, for a moment, bewildered.  Our
situation was highly interesting.  The darkness of the gale
seemed to contend with the dawn; and fancy could almost
see it hold the reins of the car of day.  The waves dashed,
our sloop ploughed the foam, many little islands reared,
through night, their ragged tops, our Captain exclaimed,
"where are we?" and all was hurly.  We were now passing over the battle waves of the gallant Perry.  Our little
gunless keel moved where whole fleets had stormed.  In
fancy's ear, the cannon's roar had not ceased to reverber-
ate; the undulating wave seemed [137] anxious to bury the

dead; the wind, through our scanty shrouds, whispered in the ear of death; and the green wave, reddened by battle, greedily sported around our sides.[91]

Many of the islands near the Bay are not larger than a dwelling-house. Their sides consist of ragged rocks, and on their summits are a few weather beaten trees.

The storm continuing, we remained at anchor in Put-in-Bay four days. During this time I frequently went ashore, and surveyed the island of this name. Wild fowl are numerous here, and in the woods there are swine. The island is uninhabited. Its soil and the growth of its timber are very good. The former abounds with limestone.

This island is rendered interesting by its forming the bay in which our fleet was moored both before and after its great victory; and also by its containing the graves of some of those who fell in the engagement. My visit to these graves excited melancholy reflections. The parade and confusion of battle had passed; and nothing was heard but the chill blast, wending its devious way through the rank weeds. So bloody was this battle, that the victor himself might well have mourned.

It was natural for me here to reflect upon our naval history. During the Revolution our prowess upon the ocean promised every thing; and in the late war even the prophecies of philosophy, and the inspirations of liberty, were distanced. But I must speak of Renown! Where

---

[91] When Perry reached Erie, Pennsylvania, to take charge of naval affairs (March, 1813), he found two vessels, the "Niagara" and the "Lawrence," already under construction. Working with tireless energy he equipped his fleet of ten vessels by August 12, and sailing up the lake anchored in Put-in-Bay to await the enemy. On the morning of September 10, the British squadron of six vessels, under Captain Barclay, appeared and the battle began. The "Lawrence," Perry's ship, being shot to pieces, he boarded the "Niagara," and again attacked the British at close range. At three in the afternoon, Barclay's two large vessels surrendered, and two others attempting to escape were captured. This victory compelled the British to evacuate Detroit.— ED.

is our Wasp ?[92]  *True* glory was her object; and she returns not for earthly honours.   Langdon and Toscin sleep
in France:[93]— they were buds of fame.   Lawrence fell,
like Hector, by the shaft of fate.[94]   My memory is full of
valour's sons; but they need not the eulogy of my pen.

In one of my excursions into the woods of Put-in-Bay
[138] island, I was accompanied by my friend Capt. W. of
the United States Army, a gentleman of a scientific and
polished mind.   Having provided ourselves with some
old clothes, we visited a cave situated about a mile from
the bay.   This cave is smaller than some others in the
west; but is, nevertheless, worth a description.

After exploring the woods for some time, we found what
we supposed might be, and what actually was the cave.
Its front is situated at the end of a considerable rise of land
of an oval form.   The mouth of the cave was very small;
and being covered with sticks and leaves, presented a very
uninviting aspect.   After removing the obstructions, we
took lights, and descending about ten feet perpendicularly,
came to a rock, the position of which was that of an in-

---

[92] The "Wasp" under command of Johnston Blakely sailed from Ports-
mouth for the British Channel (May, 1814), and began the destruction of
English merchantmen.   June 28, the brig "Reindeer" bore down upon her,
but after twenty minutes of hard fighting was compelled to surrender.   Although suffering severely in this engagement, the "Wasp" continued her rav-
ages until October, when she disappeared and was never heard from again.— Ed.

[93] Henry Langdon and Frank Toscan were both midshipmen on the "Wasp"
during her fight with the "Reindeer," and died from wounds received in the
battle.— Ed.

[94] James Lawrence, born in Burlington, New Jersey (1781), served with
Decatur in the War with Tripoli, and as lieutenant on the "Constitution."   In
1811 he was placed in command of the "Hornet," his most notable achievement
with that vessel being the destruction (1813) of the British ship "Peacock.'
For this victory he was given command of the "Chesapeake," and accepting
the challenge of the "Shannon," fought with her off Boston harbor, June, 1813.
He fell, mortally wounded, and the "Chesapeake" was compelled to surrender.
His countrymen, stirred by his dying cry, "Don't give up the ship," had his
body brought from Halifax, and buried with military honors in Trinity Church-
yard, New York City.— Ed.

clined plane. This rock is, in its descent, met by the front of the cave, so as to leave an aperture, near the floor of it, of only about three feet in length, and eighteen inches in height. This aperture also was covered with leaves. After removing them, we lay flat, and crowded ourselves, one to time, into an unknown and dismal region. As we advanced the cave, gradually, became higher; and at length we could move in an erect posture. Here we found ourselves in a spacious apartment, constituting about an acre, and surrounded by curious petrifactions. Those on the walls were small; but on the floor of the cave they were large; some of them weighing about thirty pounds. The latter are, generally of a pyramidical form. At the distance of about two hundred feet from the mouth of the cave, we came to a precipice, at the foot of which was a body of deep water. Whilst my companion sat upon the brink of the precipice, I descended it, and holding a light in one hand, swam with the other for the purpose of ascertaining the course and boundaries of this subterranean lake.

[139] In this gloomy, yet interesting cavern, we saw no living thing, excepting two bats, which were in a torpid state. Whilst exploring the most distant recesses of the cave, one of our candles was accidentally extinguished. The extinguishment of our other light would, perhaps, have been fatal to us. The darkness of this dreary region is palpable. No ray of nature's light ever visited it. Its silence too is full of thought. The slippery step of the traveller, and the stilly drippings of the slimy concave, yielded a contrast which made silence speak. Our own appearance interested us. We forgot ourselves, and unconsciously dwelt upon two ragged Fiends, prying, with taper dim, along the confines of this doleful place. We saw these beings under the low sides of the cave knocking

off some large petrifactions. We said, who are they?—
and almost shuddered to find they were ourselves.

As soon as the storm ceased we set sail from the Bay,
and the next evening arrived at Erie. In this harbour
were several United States' vessels of considerable magnitude. The banks of the harbour, on the town side, are
high, steep, and romantic; and from them there is an extensive view of the Lake. The harbour itself is spacious,
and the water deep.

At this place the celebrated General Wayne died,[95] upon
his return from his campaign against the Indians. Such
was the success of this great soldier, and such the terror
which he inspired among the savages against whom he
fought, that to this day they call him the "*sinews.*" His
mode of proceeding into the country of the enemy ought
ever to be imitated. Indians may always be defeated by
good troops, unless when the latter are ambushed, and
surprised. General Wayne proceeded with the greatest
caution during the forepart of the day, and [140] in the
afternoon employed his men in fortifying for the night; the
consequence was, that he avoided every ambuscade, ultimately met the enemy, and gave them a chastising which
made a lasting impression upon their minds.

After reaping many laurels in this campaign, General
Wayne was returning home to enjoy the grateful saluta-
tions of his fellow citizens; but death arrested him at
Erie.—

> "The path of glory leads but to the grave."

After leaving Detroit, I received a letter from the Secretary of the Lyceum there, informing me of my having, on
the evening of my departure, been admitted an honourary
member of that institution. I mention this fact for the

---

[95] General Anthony Wayne died at Erie, Pennsylvania, in December
1796.— ED.

purpose of introducing an anecdote respecting it, which was communicated to me after my return home, and which afforded me much amusement.

In passing through the country, in the early stages of my tour, some weak minded persons, who thought that my excursion was so frought with danger as to render it presumptuous, were offended by the undertaking; and adding a little ill-nature to this idea, their invectives were even more keen than the wintry winds.   One of these persons, whose common sense is like Shakspeare's grain of wheat in a bushel of chaff; and whose learning is equalled only by that of the good Mrs. Maleprop, exclaimed one day, upon seeing some newspaper, which contained an account of the Pedestrian having been admitted into the Lyceum at Detroit, ''well, they have got him into the madhouse at last!''   Mad-house? said a friend.   Yes, replied this Xenophen of the age,—''the mad-house!— the Lyceum!— all the same thing!''

[141] From Erie I proceeded to Waterford, a distance of fourteen miles.   At this place the snow upon the ground was eighteen inches deep.   The spring in the west was very backward.   I shall speak upon this topic in another place.

Waterford is a small village, and is situated on the Creek Le Beuf.   At this place is a block house, which was erected during the old French war.[96]   The Creek Le Beuf is about five miles in length, and about six rods wide.   Between this creek and French Creek, there is a little lake, covering about ten acres.   French Creek is eighty miles long, and about twenty rods in width.   This creek is one of the sources of the Alleghany river, and enters it near Fort Franklin.   The Alleghany river rises on the west of the

---

[96] For a brief history of Fort Le Bœuf, see Croghan's *Journals*, volume i of our series, note 65.— ED.

mountains of this name; and after running about two hundred miles meets the Monongahela.

The Creek Le Beuf is very crooked, and French Creek considerably so. The principal boats upon these and upon the Alleghany river are called keels. They are constructed like a whale boat, sharp at both ends; their length is about seventy feet, breadth ten feet, and they are rowed by two oars at each end. These boats will carry about twenty tons, and are worth two hundred dollars. At the stern of the boat is a stearing oar, which moves on a pivot, and extends about twelve feet from the stern. These boats move down the river with great velocity. Through the sinuosities of the narrow creek Le Beuf, the oar in the stern, by being pressed against the banks, gives to the boat a great impetus.

In going up the rivers these boats are poled. The poles are about eight feet in length, and the bottom of them enters a socket of iron, which causes the point of the pole to sink immediately. This [142] business is very laborious, and the progress of the boats slow.

The land near the creek Le Beuf and French Creek, particularly the former, is low and cold. Wild fowl are here very numerous. The lands on each side of the Alleghany river, for one hundred and fifty miles above Pittsburgh, are generally mountainous. The growth of timber here is principally white oak and chesnut, and in some places pitch pine. There are on this river some good lands, and some of a very inferior quality. But some of the best of the Pennsylvania tracts lie in the north west of the state.

The banks of the Alleghany river are, in many places, exceedingly high, steep, and rocky. Whilst moving along the current they appear stupendous. The bed of this river and of French Creek is stony, and the water of them very

clear. On these rivers are many rapids, over some of
which boats move at the rate of twelve miles an hour. In
passing down the Alleghany the scenery is delightful. The
boats move with much velocity; the country scarcely seems
inhabited; the mountains, almost lost to vision, rise in rude
majesty on both sides of the river; the pellucid aspect of
the water; the darting fish; the anxious loon; the profound
solitude, rendered more impressive by the regular dash of
the oar: all these, and many other circumstances, carry
the mind back to the days, when the original occupants
of the neighbouring wilds lived under the simple government of nature, and did not dream of the storm, which civ-
ilization was preparing for them.

On French Creek are situated Meadville, Franklin, and
several other inconsiderable places. Here too are the remains of several old forts. At Fort Franklin the French
formerly kept a garrison.[97] As [143] far down this river
as Meadville the water is still. The principal falls on this
creek and Alleghany river, are Montgomery, Patterson,
Amberson, Nichalson, and Catfish. The creeks and rivers,
which enter these waters, are numerous; but it is not
deemed worth while to name them: the principal, however, of those which enters the Alleghany are Toby's,
Sandy, Lick, Pine, and Buffalo creeks; and Crooked and
Kiskernanetas rivers.[98] In some places on the Alleghany
hills, there are fine farms. On the river is situated the little village of Armstrong; and behind the hills stands
Lawrencetown.[99] I found marching over these mountains

[97] This was Fort Venango; see Croghan's *Journals*, note 64. For Meadville,
see Harris's *Journal*, volume iii of our series, note 25.— ED.

[98] Consult Post's *Journals*, in volume i of our series, notes 22, 89, for these
rivers.— ED.

[99] Armstrong, nine miles northeast of Pittsburg, was named in honor of
Colonel John Armstrong. In 1756 he led an expedition against the Delaware
Indians who were ravaging the frontier, and destroyed their town at Kittanning.
Lawrencetown, now Lawrenceville, is two miles east of Pittsburg.— ED.

# MICHIGAN IN 1859

The following description presents specific details concerning industry, population, education and tourist attractions of the state several years before the outbreak of the Civil War.

Source: The New World in 1859 Being the United States and Canada, Illustrated and Described. New York: C. E. Baillere, Part I.

MICHIGAN, one of the more recently settled of the north-western States, occupies two peninsulas, the southern one lying between Lakes Erie, St. Clair, and Huron on the east, and Lake Michigan on the west; and the northern between Lakes Michigan and Huron on the south, and Lake Superior on the north. The whole is bounded north by Lake Superior, east by the Straits of St. Mary, Lake Huron, St. Clair River and Lake, Detroit River, and Lake Erie (all which separate it from Canada West), on the south by Ohio and Indiana, and on the west by Lakes Michigan and Wisconsin, from the latter of which it is partly separated by the Menomonee and Montreal Rivers. Michigan lies between 41° 40′ and 47° 30′ north latitude (if we exclude Isle Royale, a dependency of this State), and between 82° 12′ and 90° 30′ west longitude. The northern peninsula is about 320 miles in extreme length from south-east to north-west, and 130 in its greatest breadth, and the southern about 283 from north to south, and 210 from east to west, in its greatest width. The joint area of the two peninsulas is 56,243 square miles, or 35,595,520 acres, of which only 1,923,-582 were improved in 1850. About two-fifths of the area is included in the northern peninsula.

POPULATION.—Though originally settled by the French, the great bulk of the population is from the New England and Middle States. A large portion of the latter is of New England descent. The number of inhabitants in Michigan, in 1810, was 4762; 8896 in 1820; 31,639 in 1830; 212,267 in 1840; and 397,654 in 1850, of whom 208,471 were white males, 186,626 white females; 1412 coloured males, and 1145 coloured females.

CITIES AND TOWNS.—The towns of this State exhibit the same rapid growth which is so wonderful a characteristic of the Western States generally. Detroit, the largest town in the State, had, in 1850, a population of 21,019. The other principal towns are Ann Arbor, population, 4868; Jackson, 4147; Flint, 3304; Grand Rapids, 3147; Ypsilante, 3051; Adrian, 3006; Marshall, 2822; Pontiac, 2820; Monroe City, 2813; Tecumseh, 2679; Kalamazoo, 2507; Coldwater, 2166; and Clinton, 2130. These populations, as in New England, sometimes include the townships.

FACE OF THE COUNTRY, GEOLOGY, AND MINERALS.—The southern peninsula of Michigan, so interesting in its agricultural and economical aspects, is rather tame in its topographical features, as there is no considerable elevation (compared with the country immediately around it) within its whole extent, though the ridge which divides the waters flowing into Lakes Huron and Erie from those flowing into Lake Michigan, is 300 feet above the level of the lakes, and about 1000 above the sea. The country, however, may be generally characterized as a vast undulating plain, seldom becoming rough or broken. There are occasional conical elevations of from 150 to 200 feet in height, but generally much less. The shores of Lake Huron are often steep, forming bluffs; while those of Lake Michigan are coasted by shifting sand-hills of from 100 to 200 feet in height. In the southern part are those natural parks, thinly scattered over with trees, called, in the parlance of the country, "oak openings;" and in the south-west are rich prairie lands. The northern peninsula exhibits a striking contrast, both in soil and surface, to the southern. While the latter is level or moderately undulating, and luxuriantly fertile, the former is picturesque, rugged, and even mountainous, with streams abounding in rapids and water-falls—rich in minerals, but rigourous in climate, and sterile in soil. The Wisconsin or Porcupine Mountains which form the water-shed between Lakes Michigan and Superior, are much nearer the latter than the former, and attain an elevation of about 2000 feet in the north-west portion of the peninsula. The east part of this division of the State is undulating and picturesque, but the central hilly, and composed of table-land. The shores of Lake Superior are composed of a sandstone rock, which, in many places, is worn by the action of the wind and waves into fancied resemblances of castles, etc., forming the celebrated Pictured Rocks; while the shores of Lake Michigan are composed of a limestone rock. The streams on the northern slope of the Porcupine Mountain have a rapid descent, and abound in picturesque falls and rapids. The north peninsula is primitive, and the southern secondary; but primitive rocks are scattered over the plains of the latter of more than 100 tons weight, most abundant on the borders of the great lakes, on the flanks of valleys, and where traces of recent floods are apparent.

Michigan, in its northern peninsula, possesses, probably, the richest copper mines in the world. A block of almost pure copper, weighing some tons, and bearing the arms of the State, rests imbedded in the walls of the National Monument at Washington. The region from which this block was taken lies on the shores of Lake Superior, near the mouth of the Ontonagon River. The same mineral abounds in Isle Royale, near the north shore of Lake Superior. Iron, said to be of a very superior quality, is found in a district about 60 miles south-east of the great copper region, as well as in some other parts of Michigan. The other minerals known to exist in this State, whose mineral resources are very imperfectly developed as yet, are lead, gypsum, peat, limestone, marl, and some coal. An excellent sand for the manufacture of the finer kinds of glass-ware is found on the shores of Lake Michigan, as well as Lake Erie. The copper mines in the northern peninsula are estimated to have produced within the past year (March, 1853) nearly 4000 tons of copper, worth, on the seaboard, $1,500,000. Great activity prevails in the mining region this year; new discoveries are being made, an increased number of hands employed, and additional machinery erected. A mass of copper, weighing 5072 pounds, sent from Michigan, was exhibited at the World's Fair in New York.

OBJECTS OF INTEREST TO TOURISTS.—The Island of Mackinaw, in the straits of the same name, already visited for its picturesque beauty, may, probably, become the future Newport of the north-western States. In addition to its bold shores, rising to a height of nearly 200 feet perpendicularly above the water, and the charm of its picturesque views and cool breezes, it has the accompaniment of fine fishing in its vicinity; and the pleasant excursions to Sault St. Mary, to angle for the far-famed white fish, to tempt the sportsman and epicure to while away a summer vacation in this vicinity. About 60 miles west of the entrance of the Strait St. Marie, are the celebrated "Pictured Rocks," composed of sandstone of various colours, and worn by the action of the wind and waves into resemblances of ruined temples, castles, etc. One peculiarly striking object, called the Doric Rock, is a colonnade of 4 round pillars, of from about 3 to 7 feet in diameter, and 40 feet in height, supporting an entablature 8 feet thick, and 30 feet across. These rocks extend for about 12 miles, and rise about 300 feet above the water. Sometimes cascades shoot over the precipice, so that vessels can sail between them and the natural wall of rock. On laying out the track for a railway across the State from Detroit, the engineers encountered a singular lake, covered with an accumulation of vegetable matter—the growth of ages—but concealing beneath a deep and dangerous, though not extensive lake, which made it necessary to make a detour from the road.

CLIMATE, SOIL, AND PRODUCTIONS.—Notwithstanding the severity of the climate in Michigan, it is moderated by its proximity to the lakes; yet the temperature of the northern peninsula is quite rigourous. The northern peninsula is favourable to winter grains, but not to Indian corn; while the southern produces maize, as well as the winter grains, abundantly. The prevailing diseases are bilious fevers, ague, and dysentery: consumption is rare.

Great fertility is the characteristic of most of the soil in the middle and south of the lower peninsula; mostly free from stone, and of a deep, dark sandy loam, often mingled with gravel and clay. The northern peninsula has a large portion of rugged and poor soil, but its agricultural capabilities are not yet well developed. Portions of it are well timbered with white pine, spruce, hemlock, birch, oak, aspen, maple, ash, and elm. As the wants of the advancing settlements increase the demand, this region can furnish large supplies of lumber from its forests of pine, spruce, etc., manufactured at the fine mill-sites afforded by the rapid streams on the Superior slope of the Porcupine Mountain. Much of southern Michigan is occupied by those beautiful and fertile natural lawns, called oak openings, covered with scattered trees, and free from underwood. Another portion is prairie, and yet another timbered land, covered with black and white walnut, sugar maple, different species of oaks, hickory, ash, basswood, soft maple, elm, linden, locust, dogwood, poplar, beech, aspen, sycamore, cottonwood, cherry, pine, hemlock, spruce, tamarack, cypress, cedar, chestnut, papaw, etc. The prairies are small, and divided into wet and dry—the latter, of course, being somewhat elevated. The north-west of the lower peninsula is but little known, but recent letters from that region represent it as well timbered, well watered, and fertile; it, however, has an uninviting aspect from the lakes. On the shores of Lake Huron, near Saginaw Bay, is a marshy district. Michigan is eminently an agricultural State; the staple products being wheat, Indian corn, oats, Irish potatoes (for which it is especially favourable), butter, hay, maple sugar, wool, and live stock, with large quantities of buckwheat, rye, peas, beans, barley, fruits, cheese, beeswax, and honey; and some tobacco, sweet potatoes, wine, grass seeds, hops, flax, silk, and molasses.

MANUFACTURES.—In common with the other more recently-settled States, Michigan has not yet had leisure to give much attention to the development of her manufacturing resources. In 1850, there were in the State 1979 manufacturing establishments, each producing $500 and upwards annually, of which 15 were engaged in woollen manufactures, employing $94,000 capital, and 78 male and 51 female hands, consuming raw material worth $43,402, and producing 141,570 yards of stuffs worth $90,242; 64 forges, furnaces, etc., employing $210,450 capital, and 362 male hands, consuming raw material worth $105,865, and producing 5430 tons of castings, pig iron, etc., valued at $300,697; $139,425 capital and 98 hands were employed in the manufacture of 10,320 barrels of ale, porter, etc., and 890,900 gallons of whisky, wine, etc.; and 60 tanneries, employing $286,000 capital, consuming raw material worth $203,450, and producing manufactured leather valued at $363,980; domestic manufactures were fabricated worth $354,936.

COMMERCE.—Michigan, surrounded as it is by inland seas, is most favourably situated for internal trade, and trade with British America. Her foreign commerce is, however, small, and only amounted, in 1851–2, in imports, to $191,976, and exports, $145,152; tonnage entered for the same year, 66,041; cleared, 69,981; owned, 46,318.12, of which 24,681.73 was steam tonnage; number of vessels built, 16, with a tonnage of 2639.00. In the spring of 1853, there were owned at Detroit and Mackinaw, 56 steamers, with a tonnage of 17,925. The lake trade of 1851 has been stated at, imports, $5,330,609, and exports, $5,790,860. Wheat and other grain, flour, pork, live stock, wool, and copper are among the leading articles of export.

EDUCATION.—On the subject of education, Michigan is largely imbued with the opinion of New England (from whence so many of her sons derive their origin), that republican government and common-school education must proceed or fall together. Her school fund, in 1852, was $575,668; in addition to which, is a fund called the University Fund, of $100,000.

# BASIC FACTS

Capital City ...................... Lansing
Nickname ............... The Wolverine State
Flower ...................... Apple Blossom
Bird ............................. Robin
Tree ......................... White Pine
Song ................. *Michigan, My Michigan*
Stone ...................... Petoskey Stone
Fish .............................. Trout
Entered the Union ............ January 26, 1837

## STATISTICS*

Land Area (square miles) ............... 56,817
    Rank in Nation ...................... 22nd
Population† ...................... 9,013,000
    Rank in Nation ...................... 7th
    Density per square mile ............... 158.6
Number of Representatives in Congress ....... 19
Capital City ...................... Lansing
    Population ...................... 131,546
    Rank in State ........................ 5th
Largest City ...................... Detroit
    Population .................... 1,511,482
Number of Cities over 10,000 Population ...... 85
Number of Counties ................... 83

---

\* Based on 1970 census statistics compiled by the Bureau
of the Census.
† Estimated by Bureau of the Census for July 1, 1972.

# MAP OF CONGRESSIONAL DISTRICTS OF

# MICHIGAN

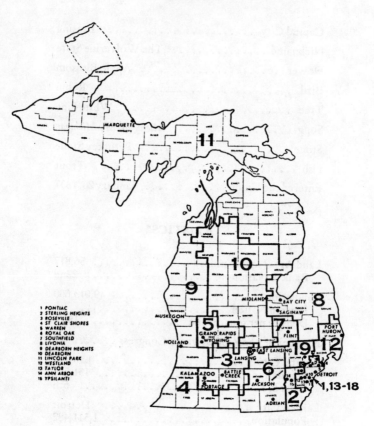

# SELECTED BIBLIOGRAPHY

Bald, Frederick Clever. Michigan in Four Centuries.
    rev. ed. New York: Harper, 1961.

Cooley, Thomas McIntyre. Michigan: A History of Govern-
    ments. Boston, N. Y.: Houghton, Mifflin and Com-
    pany, 1905.

Dunbar, Willis Frederick. Michigan: A History of the
    Wolverine State. Grand Rapids: W. B. Eerdmans
    Publishing Co., 1965.

Fuller, George Newman. Economic and Social Beginnings
    of Michigan. Lansing, Mich.: Wynkoop Hallenbeck
    Crawford Co., State Printers, 1916.

Goodrich, Calvin. The First Michigan Frontier. Ann
    Arbor: University of Michigan Press, 1940.

Russell, Nelson Vance. The British Regime in Michigan
    and the Old Northwest, 1760-1796. Northfield,
    Minn.: Carleton College, 1939.

Sarasohn, Stephen Breisman, and Vera H. Sarasohn.
    Political Party Patterns in Michigan. Detroit:
    Wayne State University Press, 1957.

Streeter, Floyd Benjamin. Political Parties in Michi-
    gan, 1837-1860. Lansing: Michigan Historical Com-
    mission, 1918.

# SELECTED BIBLIOGRAPHY

# NAME INDEX

145